Self-Publishing Essentials

Everything you need to know about self-publishing your book

VINIL RAMDEV

PublishEdge Enterprises Pvt Ltd
19/24, 1st main rd, Jayamahal, Bangalore, Karnataka, 560046 India
Email: contact@publishedge.com

www.publishedge.com

Self-Publishing Essentials by Vinil Ramdev

Print Book ISBN: 978-1-953316-09-7
Ebook ISBN: 978-1-953316-10-3

Disclaimer

Table of Contents

Introduction

Did you know that more than 1.6 million books and ebooks were published in 2018 alone?[1] More and more authors are beginning to self-publish because it gives them freedom over their content and the speed of production traditional publishers struggle to provide. Many famous authors, including Mark Twain, Michael J. Sullivan, and E. L James, self-published once upon a time.

Yet, there seem to be several myths associated with self-publishing that can be off-putting to anyone interested in doing it. For example, authors tend to think self-published books are not as good as books published by major traditional houses. But when was the last time you walked into a store and said, "I want to buy a book published by HarperCollins or Penguin, please?" I'm betting it probably never happens! Personally, I've never heard of such a thing happening. The fact is, readers don't care who publishes the book they want. Their only concerns are the author and the quality of the book. So, it doesn't matter to the reader if the book is self-published or published by a big-name publisher. Readers go after quality content and a great reading experience.

---

1   Jim Milliot, "Number of Self-Published Titles Jumped 40% in 2018," PublishersWeekly.com, October 15, 2019, https://www.publishersweekly.com/pw/by-topic/industry-news/publisher-news/article/81473-number-of-self-published-titles-jumped-40-in-2018.html.

The main reason self-published books have earned a somewhat poor reputation is because they are often of subpar quality. But why is that? The answer is simple: Self-published authors rarely use professionals to help polish their material to the same high standards demanded by traditional publishers.

I self-published my first book way back in 2009. It was an exciting journey, and I learned a lot from the experience that has stood me in good stead as both a writer and self-publisher ever since. Since then, a lot has changed, and it's much easier to publish a book today than ever before. Everything is in place for self-published authors to provide their readers with the same, and sometimes better, reading experience than the big names if they know the right way to go about it. It's really not as difficult as it might at first seem, and it needn't cost a lot of money.

My purpose in writing this book is to give readers insight into an insider's experience of the processes involved in successfully self-publishing a book that will benefit them in their own journey. I *know* a self-published book can easily be of the same quality as one published by a big-name publisher. Within these chapters, I go step-by-step through all the necessary processes involved in successfully self-publishing a high-quality book.

After reading this book, readers will be able to self-publish a professional quality paperback, ebook, or audiobook with confidence and ease. I also cover marketing and selling books. Authors tend to forget that no one can buy their books if they don't know they're out there ready to purchase! I show readers how, besides merely publishing, authors can also find ways to promote their book and ensure their target readers know about it.

Before we start, I'd like to say how much I've enjoyed writing this book. Considering I self-published my first book back in 2009, it has been quite a learning experience throughout the years since then. Putting decades of learning experiences into one book has been laborious yet heart-warming. As you will discover, self-publishing a book is exciting, and I encourage you to enjoy the journey.

Chapter 1

What is Publishing?

Publishing is generally referred to as the act of making your book available for sale. When we talk about publishing, we generally mean the traditional publishing model, where we, the author, approach a publisher. If they decide to publish our book, they will do so in exchange for a royalty. Royalty is the term used to describe a percentage of the amount made from a book's sales. The publisher keeps a certain percentage, and you, the author, are given a certain percentage from the amount earned through the book's sales. Different publishers calculate royalties differently. Some calculate them based on net sales, while others look at retail sales. Briefly, net sales refers to the total sales figure without deductions. Retail, or gross sales, means the total sales figure will have deductions made for allowances, discounts, and returns made at the retail point. It's essential for authors to be aware of the finer details of any contract to see how their royalties are calculated.

In the traditional publishing option, it's your publisher's job to ensure your book is distributed and available at bookstores, online retailers, libraries, and academic institutions. But that is merely *distribution* and not *marketing*. Many people think a traditional publisher will do all the marketing for them, but that is not necessarily the case with all companies. True, many large traditional publishing houses have dedicated marketing departments to handle book publicity, but with self-publishing, marketing is the author's job.

If you don't want to spend time and energy searching for a traditional publisher, you can be your own publisher and publish the book yourself. This is what is popularly called *self-publishing*.

Self-publishing is much easier today than ever before because of the many custom-designed platforms that have made distributing a self-published book simple. Many of these platforms are free or cost very little to sign up for and publish your book.

All you need to do is sign up for one of these platforms and purchase an ISBN (International Standard Book Number); some even provide free ISBNs. Then, you simply fill up your tax info, upload your book files, and wait for the self-publishing platform to approve the book files and distribute them to thousands of online retailers and bookstores.

Difference between Traditional Publishing and Self-Publishing

Traditional publishing is one of the earliest forms of publishing. When a publishing house purchases the copyright to a writer's work in exchange for royalties, it is typically referred to as traditional publishing. In this scenario, an author, or the author's agent, generally pitches to a publishing house with a book proposal, which is an outline of a book to be written. If the publishing house accepts the book proposal, the writer then writes the manuscript, which goes through several changes based on the book editor's feedback, and, eventually, the publisher publishes and distributes the book.

Self-publishing, as the name indicates, is when the author is the publisher. The author takes full responsibility for the publishing process. The typical self-publishing process includes writing, hiring an editor to edit and proofread your work, designing your book cover and book interior, and signing up and getting your book files approved on one of the many self-publishing platforms.

The biggest advantage to the author in traditional publishing is the cost.

The author generally pays nothing to get their book published: the editing, design, production, and distribution of the book is entirely the publisher's responsibility. However, in return for these services, the author forgoes a substantial amount of the royalties earned by book sales. In the traditional publishing model, an author typically gets just 4–10 percent of the book sales in royalties. If the author is famous and sales are likely to be high, a publishing company will often pay an advance against royalties. So, as you can see, the value of traditional publishing depends a lot on the deal. Some deals are great, while others . . . not so much!

On the other hand, self-publishing can be expensive if you use qualified professionals along the way to ensure high quality. However, the author keeps 100 percent of the book's profits because they have no publisher to share it with. Some authors try to do everything themselves. If you have great editing and design skills, you might just get away with it. But, in my experience, if you're a first-time author and are serious about producing a good quality book, it's essential to use seasoned professionals to support you.

In traditional publishing, the full rights to the author's work belong to the publisher. The author cannot repurpose their content or use it anywhere without the publisher's permission. However, a self-published author has complete control over their work. They can use the content in any way they like.

The traditional publishing process can be time-consuming. It can take over twelve months before your book is published. Self-publishing is the fastest way to get published. If your manuscript is ready, you can publish it in less than a few weeks. I know some self-published authors who publish one book a month. It might sound impossible to some people, but if an author writes 8,000 words a day, that's 160,000 words in twenty days. Add another ten days for editing—and that's one book a month. Many of us may not have the time to achieve that, but we can still write 300–500 words a day and knock out two books a year. That's four times more books than a traditional publisher will publish in two years!

One of the biggest myths in the publishing world is that traditional publishers will do the author's marketing, from setting up interviews with big-time talk shows to getting them shelf-space in big chain bookstores. Unfortunately, as I've already mentioned, that's not always true. Traditional publishers focus on books that make them money. If your book doesn't make them money, you are pretty much all by yourself. The money makers for a traditional publisher are less than 10 percent of their titles. The other 90 percent barely sell any copies. Traditional publishers are attracted to authors who already have their marketing in place. If an author does not already have an audience (fan base), they are unlikely to attract a traditional publisher.

If a traditional publisher does not do the marketing for you, and you already have an audience, it's obvious you'll make a lot more money by keeping all the royalties to yourself. For example, if a traditional publisher offers you 6 percent royalties for a book that retails at $10, that's $0.60 per sale. On the other hand, as a self-published author, you'll probably keep $3 or more for every sale. So, you make the same amount of money if you sell 5,000 books from a traditional publishing deal or 1,000 books as a self-published author. That's an astonishing difference, I'm sure you'll agree!

Many people ask me if they should pursue a traditional publishing deal or self-publish. Well, for most people, a traditional publishing deal is not an option. It takes several years of pitching to publishers before you land a publishing deal. Even after that, there is no guarantee your book will sell. I've heard stories of many authors who were rejected by hundreds of publishers. Based on my experience, instead of investing time and effort in chasing a traditional publishing deal, most first-time authors would probably be better off spending the same amount of energy on building their own author platform. I'll tell you more about this in later chapters.

Vanity Publishing

Many authors write to publishers with the hope of getting a traditional publishing deal. They hear a positive response and are excited. However, after a few email exchanges, the publisher asks the author to make a payment. In a traditional publishing deal, the author will never be asked to pay. However, if the company provides self-publishing services, then the author pays for the editing, design, and typesetting services.

If publishers charge money to publish your book, it's no different than self-publishing. The difference is merely in the form of communication. Vanity publishers will rave about the quality of your manuscript and how great it is and then ask you to contribute to the book's production costs, generally tens of thousands of dollars. It's not uncommon for authors to be charged $12,000—$35,000 for the book's production. Sometimes, authors pay tens of thousands of dollars and still get to keep only 10 percent of the book's sales because of the terms of the contract they signed with the vanity publisher.

Sometimes, companies try to incorporate some features of self-publishing and traditional publishing into a hybrid model. Authors pay 50 percent of the production costs and keep 50 percent of the profits from the book.

Subsidy publishing or vanity press are other names given to this kind of vanity publishing. But not every vanity press is a scam, unethical, or corrupt. Some such schemes might work for certain authors but not for others. Whether you use a vanity press, self-publishing, hybrid, or traditional publishing, it's essential that authors understand what they're getting into. Make sure you know the ins and outs, the benefits, and pitfalls of it before investing your time and money. Read the contract several times before signing and paying any money.

Whether you opt for a traditional publisher, self-publishing, or a vanity publisher, be clear about what you're signing up for. Self-publishing is much easier than ever before, and it costs far less in comparison to vanity publishing. Several publishing services companies offer services as good as or better than vanity publishers for a much lower price. So, self-publishing might be a far better option than paying exorbitant amounts of money to a vanity publisher. In the next chapter, I'll show you a step-by-step process for successfully self-publishing your book.

Chapter 2

Step-by-Step Process to Self-Publishing

If you are looking to self-publish your book, remember you are going to be doing all the tasks a traditional publisher would do for you. This includes editing, cover design, typesetting (designing your paperback's interior pages and formatting your ebook), and distribution.

Once you have the first draft of your manuscript ready, your next step is editing and proofreading. To help you, I have outlined a step-by-step process to self-publishing your book.

Step 1: Editing and Proofreading

Many self-published books look self-published because authors haven't taken the time to edit their books. Even the world's best authors use a professional editor. Even though professional editors can be expensive, they are worth their weight in gold. One of the biggest reasons self-published books struggle to sell is because of the quality of the content. An unedited book looks unedited because it *is* unedited. Editing can be time-consuming and requires a good knowledge of important details like correct spelling, grammar, and punctuation. A good editor can make your book look professional and as good as one published by a traditional publisher.

Step 2: Book Cover

The old saying "Don't judge a book by its cover" doesn't hold true in publishing. As readers, we all know we're initially attracted by the book cover. Therefore, your book cover plays a vital role in influencing the sales of your book. A good cover may not sell a bad book, but a great cover can sell a good book. Some designers specialize in book covers, and book covers need to have specific things included in their design to be successful. Here's a basic checklist of what makes a good book cover.

The title should be clear and legible

The title on the book cover needs to be legible and easy to read. I have seen many book covers that are super-creative, but it's still hard to make out the book's actual title. Aesthetics is great, but what is the point of aesthetics if the title itself is not legible? The first thing people look for and should see straight away on the cover is the title of the book. If the title itself is not readable, it will not be memorable, and people will simply forget it when they are ready to buy. The fonts used for the title should be of a type that ensures it is clearly readable and easy on the eyes.

The cover should be clutter-free

Personally, I like covers that are clutter-free, and experience tells me this works best when trying to attract buyers. I don't recommend using colors so bright that they are distracting and difficult on the eyes. It's best to ensure the colors on the cover are compatible and the text easily legible. There are so many things we can add to the cover. A print paperback cover has a front cover, spine, and back cover. The front cover has the title, subtitle, and the author's name on it. The spine generally has the book title and author's name on it. Sometimes it includes a publisher's logo. Since the spine doesn't have much space on it, the information it contains is limited. The back cover has a little bit more information on it. The back cover generally includes a book description (known as the blurb), information about the author, and a testimonial. The purpose of the back cover is to entice the reader to buy the book. When someone wants to buy a book at a bookstore, once they're attracted by the front cover and title, they generally look at the book's back cover before any other part of the book. It's like checking out the trailer to a movie. If we like the trailer of the movie, we'll probably pay to watch it. It's the same with the back cover of a book: if we like the description, we may very well decide to buy it. Some authors write a synopsis or a book description on the back cover. I've also seen people use just testimonials. There's no right or wrong when it comes to deciding what information you should add to the back cover. My only advice is to add anything you think increases the probability of selling the book.

An ebook generally features just the front cover of the book. The contents of the back cover can be tweaked and added to the product page.

The cover for an audiobook is usually square in shape, as compared to a vertical rectangle for an ebook. A good designer can resize your ebook's front cover into a square shape that can be used to publish the audiobook version.

Step 3: Typesetting

Typesetting is the term used for designing the interior pages of the book. It involves laying out the words in an organized manner on the page so they are structured correctly into well-spaced paragraphs and are easy to read. When you open a book, you see the title page, the copyright page, the table of contents, the chapter title, headers, and page numbers laid out in an organized manner. Good typesetting is subtle; it doesn't and shouldn't stand out, but its presence enhances the reader's experience. The most important part of the typesetting procedure is ensuring the text is easy to read.

In the chapter on paperbacks, I discuss book dimensions, typesetting a paperback book, and the options available. In the ebook chapter, I talk about formatting an ebook.

Step 4: Distribution

Once you have your book cover and interior files ready, it is time to distribute your book. As I have already mentioned in the previous chapter, it's much easier to self-publish your book today than ever before. All you need to do is upload your book cover and interior files onto a distribution platform (or aggregator), and it will distribute your book to thousands of retailers and online partners. You will need an ISBN if you want to distribute your book. Some online distribution platforms offer an ISBN free of cost, but you can only use it on their platform. If you want to use a single ISBN on all distribution platforms to maintain uniformity in the ISBN, it's best to purchase an ISBN. It's fairly simple to do this, and I explain in detail how and why to buy an ISBN in future chapters.

In this chapter, I have given you a basic overview summarizing the self-publishing process, but I cover all these aspects in more detail in subsequent chapters.

Chapter 3

Print Books

If someone asked you to define what we mean when we say 'a book,' what would be your answer?

Before the digital era, we'd call anything bound by sheets of paper a book. According to Merriam-Webster's dictionary, a book is "a set of written sheets of skin or paper or tablets of wood or ivory."[2]

Today, those tablets are long gone, and while many books are still published on paper sheets, a vast number are now produced in digital form—the ebook. Merriam-Webster defines this modern form as "a book composed or converted into digital format for display on a computer or a handheld device."[3] Such devices include smartphones, tablets, etc. So, any written matter gathered together in a set of pages, whether it's a fictional narrative or a set of instructions on how to do something, we can call a book. We might like to believe the days of print are over because it is so much more convenient to access an ebook. For example, if you

---

2   "Book," Merriam-Webster (Merriam-Webster), accessed August 28, 2021, https://www.merriam-webster.com/dictionary/book.

3   "E-Book," Merriam-Webster (Merriam-Webster), accessed August 28, 2021, https://www.merriam-webster.com/dictionary/e-book.

download the Kindle™ app on your phone, you can access thousands of books via your phone without having to physically carry them wherever you go.

It's like carrying thousands of books in your pocket, except they're as light as a feather! Even as little as fifty years ago, I doubt anyone could have imagined being able to carry thousands of books about with them in their pockets.

And it's all thanks to the powerful world of technology we live in today.

Nevertheless, over the years, my conversations with people have led me to believe there is still a major market for print books, and the numbers bear this out.

According to market statisticians Statista, the average annual number of print books sold in the US is 675 million. Estimates show that 335.7 million ebooks were sold in 2019.[4] It's hard to track the exact numbers, but it's safe to say that ebooks have made a healthy dent in the overall book market. But they aren't about to kill off the demand for print books!

About 20 percent of readers in a recent survey stated that they prefer ebooks over print books, but the vast majority still prefer print books.[5]

Statista publishing industry figures also state 689.5 million print books were sold in the US in 2019.[6] In 2004, 648 million print books were sold. It seems, therefore, that sales of print books have been fairly consistent

---

4   Amy Watson, "Topic: E-Books," Statista, accessed August 28, 2021, https://www.statista.com/topics/1474/e-books/#dossierSummary.

5   "Print Books vs. e-Books: What's the Future of Reading?" SurveyMonkey, accessed August 28, 2021, https://www.surveymonkey.com/curiosity/print-books-vs-e-books-whats-the-future-of-reading/.

6   Amy Watson, "Topic: E-Books," Statista

in the last fifteen years. The Association of American Publishers' 2019 annual report mentions that annual revenue earned by the sale of ebooks has actually decreased slightly since 2018 to 2.6 percent compared to revenues of 74.7 percent from print book sales in the same year.[7] So, as you can see, the print book market is still quite healthy. I have even come across many young people in their twenties who still prefer a print book. A recent survey by the Bookseller of 1,000 readers aged between sixteen and twenty-four showed that 64 percent said they prefer print books to ebooks.[8] So, these figures suggest that print books are still going strong, and I believe the market for print books will stay strong for many years to come.

History of Books

If we want to identify when the first book was created, we need to go back to when scripts were first invented. Experts in the field theorize that scripts were developed by people only from around 3400 BC, starting in ancient Mesopotamia.[9] This is fairly recent in comparison to the proposed lifetime of the human race—approximately six million years.[10] If we were to look at that period as if it were twenty-four hours measured on a clock, then scripts have been around for only seventy-five seconds.

---

7 "AAP StatShot Annual REPORT: Book Publishing Revenues up Slightly TO $25.93 Billion in 2019," AAP, July 31, 2020, https://publishers.org/news/aap-statshot-annual-report-book-publishing-revenues-up-slightly-to-25-93-billion-in-2019/.

8 Charlotte Eyre, "Young People Prefer Print to e-Books," The Bookseller (The Bookseller, September 30, 2015), https://www.thebookseller.com/news/young-people-prefer-print-e-books-313321#.

9 "History of Writing," Wikipedia (Wikimedia Foundation, August 21, 2021), https://en.wikipedia.org/wiki/History_of_writing.

10 Elizabeth Howell, "How Long Have Humans Been on Earth?" Universe Today, December 23, 2015, https://www.universetoday.com/38125/how-long-have-humans-been-on-earth/.

SELF-PUBLISHING ESSENTIALS

Although there is much debate among historians about the accuracy of these dates, they nevertheless show the advent of written scripts to be quite recent in the history of our development.

It is said by experts that human beings once communicated mostly by using their bodies, through gestures and sounds. Later, we developed a language that was primarily verbal. Eventually, scripts came along to record that spoken language, so it could be read and understood by others.

Chinese, Tamil, Sanskrit, Hebrew, and Arabic are among some of the oldest written languages that still survive today.[11]

The earliest forms of writing used symbols to express ideas or state information, as can be seen clearly in ancient Egyptian hieroglyphics.

Papyrus, wood, and bronze were some of the earliest mediums of writing before paper.[12] During the middle-ages, books were written by hand, mostly by monks in religious institutions. And if more copies of the same book were needed, they had to be copied by hand. So, books were expensive, and only the wealthy could afford them.[13]

---

11   Geoffrey Migiro, "Oldest Languages Still in Use Today," WorldAtlas (WorldAtlas, January 28, 2020), https://www.worldatlas.com/articles/oldest-languages-still-in-use-today.html.

12   "HISTORY OF WRITING MATERIALS," History World, accessed August 29, 2021, http://www.historyworld.net/wrldhis/plaintexthistories.asp?historyid=aa92.

13   Department of Medieval Art and The Cloisters. "The Art of the Book in the Middle Ages." In Heilbrunn Timeline of Art History. New York: The Metropolitan Museum of Art, 2000–. http://www.metmuseum.org/toah/hd/book/hd_book.htm (October 2001)

A process called block printing was initially developed to print entire books. The Diamond Sutra,[14] accepted as one of the oldest printed books, is known to have used this method. Blocks of wood were carved, and ink was smeared into the carved areas and stamped onto paper to create an image.[15] Block printing is still used in some parts of the world, not to print books but to create designs on fabric.

Later, other forms of printing like screen printing and lithography developed. Screen printing, which is still used today in artworks and textile printing, involves creating a stencil over a mesh.[16] It was used to create type-like figures by blocking certain parts of the stenciled image while leaving others open. Once the ink was drawn over the stencil and the stencil removed, the ink remaining on the page surface appeared as a typed letter, symbol, or image. Screen printing was used to create business cards as recently as the early nineties.

The most notable printing invention was the Gutenberg Press in 1450, which mass-produced the Bible.[17] It was perhaps one of the first pieces of literary work that was not copied by hand.

14   "Diamond Sutra," Wikipedia (Wikimedia Foundation, July 28, 2021), https://
en.wikipedia.org/wiki/Diamond_Sutra.

15   "Block Printing," Encyclopædia Britannica (Encyclopædia Britannica, Inc.),
accessed August 29, 2021, https://www.britannica.com/technology/block-
printing.

16   Catherine Sullivan, "History of Screen Printing," California State University
Chico, 2011, https://www.csuchico.edu/turner/_assets/documents/
history-of-screen-printing.pdf.

17   "The Gutenberg Press," Encyclopædia Britannica (Encyclopædia Britannica,
inc.), accessed August 29, 2021, https://www.britannica.com/topic/
printing-publishing/The-Gutenberg-press.

How Did the Gutenberg Press Work?

Gutenberg's press made books affordable for even the middle class, which increased the literacy levels of people across the world.

Gutenberg's press created a movable type, with individual letters or symbols fitted into a wooden plate. Ink was then spread over the plate, and paper was placed on it. A second plate pressed the paper down over the lower plate, which resulted in a duplication of the letters onto the paper. This was one of the early forms of printing. I'd wonder why we called it a printing 'press,' but now I understand: it's because the inked type is 'pressed' against the paper, thereby duplicating the desired letters or images. The Gutenberg Press could print about 250 pages per hour.

In 1796, German author Alois Senefelder invented lithography, which used oil, water, and ink, as a cheap way to print theatrical works.[18] It used a plain material, for instance, limestone, as the plate, and grease or oil ink was applied to the plate. Then, the paper was pressed against the plate, which absorbed the ink. The type prepared without grease was not copied to the paper because water repels ink.

Offset Printing

Paper mill owner Ira Rubel accidentally discovered 'offset lithography.'[19] He discovered that by transferring the image from the lithography stone to a rubber blanket, the images appeared sharper. He then, along with another printer, created a press where the image would first be transferred to a rubber blanket and then onto (offset) paper. Offset

---

18 "Lithography," Wikipedia (Wikimedia Foundation, July 11, 2021), https://en.wikipedia.org/wiki/Lithography.

19 Ibid.

printing today has become the most common printing method for printing in bulk quantities.

However, if you are looking to print smaller quantities of books, then offset printing can become very expensive. The printer must first prepare the plates, which is labor-intensive and time-consuming (and so entails a high upfront cost). Offset may not be an option if you are printing less than 1,000 copies because the upfront costs might turn out to be expensive. This is the point where the game became difficult for the smaller, independent publishers and self-published authors. However, things improved radically for smaller players in the last decade when 'print-on-demand' leveled the playing field between them.

Print-on-Demand

Today, print-on-demand has dramatically changed the way book publishing works. In fact, the technology which enables print-on-demand has drastically changed the way book publishing works. If you want to print, say, just one book, then offset printing would be prohibitively expensive. The upfront cost is high, making it impractical for producing small numbers of copies. So, what happens when you *do* want to print just one book? Well, offset printing requires a print run of at least 1,000 copies for it to be economically viable. However, with print-on-demand, you can print just one book, and there's no upfront cost for creating the plates—because there are no plates involved. Instead, print-on-demand uses an imaging technology quite different from anything that came before.

How has this changed the way books are published and sold? A major change is that online retailers no longer need to maintain a physical inventory of books. They can print books once a customer places an order for a specific book. Almost all online bookstores print books on-demand, which means that when a customer purchases your book, only then is it printed and shipped. This method saves a lot of money for self-published authors because they don't need to predict sales, do stock inventory, or pay for printing upfront. The upfront costs of printing now no longer exist for a self-published author. So, with most books being bought online nowadays, self-published authors can at last compete with the big publishers.

Print-on-demand uses digital technology. It does not use plates as in offset printing. Images are transferred to paper using laser imaging technology. Related technology has also dramatically improved in the last few years, and the quality of a modern inkjet printer is as good as that of offset printing.

The print quality depends on the type of ink, the paper, and how the ink is transferred onto paper.

Inkjet and toner printing are popular forms of digital printers. Toner printing is the type you see produced by copying machines, where the print comes out in rich shades of back and has sharper edges. Inkjet printing has finer resolution and more vibrant colors.

The type of ink used differs from machine to machine. Each machine has its own compatible inks. Some inks are dry, and others wet. Resolution and sharpness depend on the type of nk being used.

Types of Paper

Paper is one of the most important raw materials required to produce a print book. The pages of almost all modern print books are made of paper, not silk or papyrus, as in earlier times. But, as you will know, not all paper is the same. There are many different types of paper. The next time you walk into a bookstore, try looking through several different books on the bookshelves, and you'll find various sorts of paper being used.

The most common difference you'll notice is between white and cream paper. Then, there are varying weights of paper, measured in GSM or gram per square meter. There's also acid-free paper. The benefit of acid-free paper is that it doesn't turn yellow over time and lasts longer. There is also coated and uncoated paper.

Coated paper is coated and polished with an agent to make the surface smooth, giving it either a matte or glossy finish. The coating does not allow the paper to absorb the ink, which makes the images sharper and brighter. Coated paper is mostly used for book covers rather than the interior pages of the book. Glossy finish on coated paper gives it a shiny finish, while the matte finish is less shiny. Some authors prefer a shiny finish, while others prefer a less shiny finish. Matte gives a more natural look to the book cover. Glossy gives a sharper contrast and makes the book cover look brighter. Whether one uses a glossy or matte finish is a matter of choice. Simply walking into a bookstore and exploring both glossy and matte covers will allow you to figure out which option you prefer.

Uncoated paper does not have any coating on the surface. The paper is generally rougher and more porous than coated paper. The print will appear less crisp and will have a softer feel when compared to coated paper. The interior pages of almost all print books use uncoated paper. Uncoated paper comes in smooth and vellum finishes. The next time you open a print book, run your hands across the paper, and you'll feel either a smooth finish or a rough vellum finish where the fibers stick out of the paper. Text and images will look sharper on the smooth finish compared to the vellum. Some people still prefer the vellum finish because it gives a more antique finish to the book.

Difference Between Cream and White Paper

One of the most visible differences in paper you'll observe is in its color. Some books have white paper, while others have cream paper. Amazon direct publishing provides you with the option of either #55 (90 GSM) white or cream paper. Although white and cream are the same weight, 90 GSM, the cream paper is marginally thicker and will make your spine look a little thicker. Still, whether you opt for white or cream is a matter of choice.

I prefer cream paper because it feels warmer and softer and is easier on the eyes compared to white paper. An interior designer friend of mine equates white light with industrial lighting, and this stark effect is what you get when you opt for using white paper in your book interior compared with the warmer, easy-on-the-eye cream color. But again, it's a matter of choice rather than convention, tradition, or functionality. Bearing this in mind, your choice might also be influenced by the content of your book. For instance, I think white paper gives a more formal and serious feel to a book, while cream paper gives it a warmer, softer feel. So, if your book is on a highly technical subject, then white paper might work for you, but if it contains a fictional narrative, cream may be the best choice. Again, the cover design also adds to the overall appeal of the book, and the uniformity of the whole depends on the look and feel of the book. So, uniformity in the book's appearance and feel is an aspect to consider when deciding which color paper to use.

Binding

The main purpose of binding is to protect books from wear and tear, dust, and moisture.

Once upon a time, binding was done in a 'bindery.' Printers would print the book on paper and send it to a bindery, where the books would either be sewed or stitched together and bound with the book cover. Today, several printers do the book binding in-house.[20]

History of Book Binding

Like other aspects of book production, binding has evolved over several centuries. What follows is a basic history of the binding methods that have been used over several centuries.

Palm Leaves by Monks

If we look back at history and how books were first bound, we can see how, around 100 BC, palm leaves were used instead of paper, as early monks would bind the palm leaves with twine. The earliest method of binding can be seen in ancient scrolls, where the papyrus sheets bearing the text would simply be rolled up into a tube around a rod. Each sheet would be unrolled to read the content. Then, the Romans came up with the 'codex' (plural: codices), which featured a stack of loose pages bound together, and which made reading much easier.[21] The codex closely resembles the modern form of binding we know today.

Scrolls

Scrolls feature one of the first forms of binding methods used around the world. Sheets of papyrus or paper were rolled around a core material,

---

20 "Bookbinding," Wikipedia (Wikimedia Foundation, August 26, 2021), https://en.wikipedia.org/wiki/Bookbinding.

21 "Ancient Romans Invented the First Bound Book," Ancient Pages, September 25, 2017, https://www.ancientpages.com/2017/09/25/ancient-romans-invented-first-bound-book/.

just like paper towels are rolled up today. One literally scrolled up the sheet, and when someone wanted to read the text, they would simply unroll it. Scrolls aren't often produced today, except for specific reasons. For instance, scrolls are used in some religious ceremonies or as props in historical films.

Codex

Since scrolls were inconvenient, the Romans came up with the codex method, where single sheets of papyrus were folded and bound together. This made reading much more convenient than with scrolls, especially when there were large amounts of content to be recorded.

Leather

Leather remains one of the most common binding materials used around the world. Even today, some books still use leather. The reason is because leather is very durable and protects the contents of a book from humidity, wear and tear, and other damage. Paper lasts for only a few years if kept in the right conditions and can be easily damaged due to humidity and several other factors. However, leather made from animal skin lasts longer. Properly prepared animal skin can last for several thousand years. For centuries, the British parliament has recorded its laws on 'vellum' instead of paper. Vellum is a very thin form of animal skin specially prepared to be written on. Some ancient books written on vellum and bound with a leather cover have lasted for thousands of years.

Today, the British parliament still records its laws on vellum, even if vellum is extremely expensive compared to paper. Vellum is generally made from calf skin. The biggest advantage of vellum and leather over paper is that, stored well, books can last for thousands of years without showing signs of too much wear and tear.

Metal

Besides leather, other materials and styles, like metal, wood, pastelboards, dust jacket-like paper wrappers, cloth, case bindings, and flap-style paper dust jackets have all made their way into the book binding process. Some books are even stitched down the middle instead of using glue.

Modern Binding: How is Binding Done Today?

Book production has dramatically changed today, mostly due to economic reasons. The most common type of book found today is a paperback or a hardcover.

A paperback has a soft cover made of thick paper. A hardcover's book cover is made of cardboard and cloth and is much thicker. The paper inside a hardcover book is usually much thicker and of a higher premium quality than in a paperback. It is usually bound by staples and stitching. A paperback is bound by glue and is more likely to tear or get bent along the edges more easily than a hardcover.

A hard cover is a premium version of the book, whereas the paperback is a budget-friendly version. Hardcovers are more durable than paperbacks because of the dust-free coating they have applied to them. Hardcovers are often used for gifting purposes or by those who prefer something more substantial and durable for their bookshelves.

It seems obvious, then, that hardcovers have a much higher production cost than paperbacks. If, for example, you want to give away books for free at a conference, then the paperback format will undoubtedly save you a lot of money in comparison to hardback.

Not all self-publishing platforms give you a hardcover option. So, if you're certain you want to go with a hardcover, then opt for a self-publishing platform that offers you that option.

Print Book Dimensions

Print books come in various dimensions. 6x9", 5.5x8.5", and 5x8" are the most common ones. Depending on the length of your book, you can choose a size that works best for you. For instance, as a rough guide, if your book is 36,000 words or less, then a 5x8" might work best for you because those dimensions will prevent the book from looking too thin. However, if you choose to go with a 6x9", then the number of pages is reduced, which reduces the cost of printing as well.

A 5x8" is a handy size that fits into most bags. However, it does increase the number of pages, and so printing costs will be higher compared to a 6x9". Most of my books are shorter, so I stick to 5.5x8.5". It's worth checking what sizes the different self-publishing platforms offer. For instance, Lulu does not have the option to publish a 5'x8'.[22]

I prefer sticking to either 5.5x8.5" or 6x9" because these sizes are available on most self-publishing platforms. If I do decide to publish someplace else, I don't need to resize and typeset my book all over again.

Typesetting

Imagine opening a print book. You see words and sentences arranged in a particular order. There is a header, footer, page numbers, etc. Some books have a header with the book title on one page and the author's name on the other, while others have the book title on one page and

---

22   "Lulu," Lulu, accessed August 29, 2021, https://www.lulu.com/.

the chapter title on the other. However, there's no specific requirement set down about the layout. Each book designer uses their own style and process to design the interior of the book. Each chapter has a style— for example, in the manner the chapter title is written. Some chapters might open with a drop font or other effect at the beginning of each new chapter's text.

The process of laying out the words on a page, choosing the right font and font size, choosing the way the chapter title is written, and the way the chapter begins are decisions made by the typesetter.

The typesetter's job is to ensure a clean and well-organized design that enhances the reader experience.

Some of the decisions made by the typesetter include:

#1 Drop Font: The first letter of the chapter is usually in a bigger font than the rest of the text, which is intended mostly for decorative purposes. The purpose of good design is to provide a good reader experience.

#2 Chapter Title: The title of the chapter is usually written in a slightly different and more immediately striking way compared to the rest of the text—because we want the chapter title to stand out.

#3 Font and Font-Size: Today, there are hundreds of different fonts available for us to use when producing our own books. The majority of these fonts have been created to make the text on the interior pages easily readable, while some are merely for decorative purposes. Ebooks usually have bigger fonts than print books because they make it easier to read the text on a device. On the other hand, print books have fonts that, in addition to providing a good reader experience, should also take up less space so that the number of pages reduces, thereby also reducing printing costs. With print books, it's vital that print costs should

be taken into consideration. If we use bigger fonts, the number of pages can increase, which will also increase the cost of printing. So, when designing print books, keep printing costs in mind as well. The font size can dramatically increase the cost of printing, which can mean you have to increase the selling price of the book. Therefore, it can reduce the profitability of your book. Try to choose a font and size that lets you find a balance between providing readers with a good experience and keeping printing costs down. An ideal font size is one where reader experience is not compromised, but printing costs are not dramatically increased. Experiment and try to find that balance for your book.

#4 *Spacing Between Sentences:* Again, too much spacing between sentences can increase the number of pages, thereby increasing printing costs. Single spacing can still work well, depending on the font and font size. Double spacing clearly increases the number of pages needed by two, but a 1.5-spacing bridges the gap between single and 1.5 and offers a good alternative where you think it will be beneficial for the reader. According to the font and font size, the typesetter can create an ideal spacing for your book. The most important thing is for the text to be easily legible and readable. If sentences are too close together, they may be difficult to read. It may be handy to know that in design language, the vertical space, or the distance between the bottom of the words and the top of the words in the sentence just below it is called 'leading.'

#5 *Headers:* The headers on a print book are not the same on every page. The headers on the odd pages can differ from those on the even pages. For instance, you may have noticed that some typesetters place the author's name on one side of the page and the chapter title on the other, along with the page number. But again, there are no hard and fast rules on what should go where; designers will add information where they think it is most likely to benefit the reader, or for decorative purposes.

Page numbers are more important in a print book than an ebook because they give the reader direction.

#6 Footers: Page numbers are found either in the footer or header of each page. If the page number is in the header of the page, then the footer can be used to add any additional information, like the name of a website, or can even be left blank. I usually like the page number to be in the footer and the header to have the book title on the even page and chapter title on the odd page. Some people put the author's name on the odd page and the book title on the even page. This is a subtle way of emphasizing both the book title and the author's name separately.

#7 Margins: Margins are the spaces at the top, bottom, and the sides of a page. The margins should not be too close to the edge of a page because when the person cutting the print book cuts it too close, some of the letters on the page could get cut off. The margin on one side of the page will be slightly more than on the other because the typesetter will take account of the part of the page to be glued to the binding. If the margins are too close to the binding, the reader might find it hard to read the text. That is why typesetters leave some space for the binding.

#8 Gutter: The margin closest to the spine is called the gutter. It's best to leave a little extra bit of space in the inside margins to take account of the book binding process. If the margins are too small, the text might appear too close to the bind, and readers might struggle to read it. So, keep that in mind, and make the gutters—the inside margins—just wide enough, so the text is not too close to the binding.

#9 Bleed: When images, text, or other elements of your book extend beyond the margins, then it is called 'bleed.' Bleed is when there is no white space in the margins. Most of my books have no bleed. If you choose to use bleed in your books, make sure your designer knows what

they're doing. If it's a non-fiction book with no images, I suggest not using bleed.

#10 Tracking: Tracking is the term used to describe the space between letters. We want the space between letters to be consistent. They can be increased or decreased, provided they look in sync and are easily readable.

#11 Kerning: While tracking adjusts the spacing between a range of letters, 'kerning' is about adjusting the space between individual characters. Sometimes, depending on the font, the letters A and W might seem too close to each other. The typesetter may have to move the characters slightly to make them look uniform.

#12 Orphans and Widows: Many self-published books that are not properly typeset will have 'widows and orphans.' A widow is when the last sentence or word from a paragraph on the previous page ends up on the following page all by itself. So, when you see a single sentence or word from the paragraph on the previous page dangling on the top of the page by itself, that's called a widow.

An orphan, on the other hand, is a sentence from the beginning of a paragraph that is dangling alone at the bottom of the page.

It's common for a paragraph to start at the bottom of the page or end just at the beginning of the page. When a typesetter sees these things, they can make minor adjustments to ensure there is no single sentence hanging by itself at the bottom or at the beginning of the page.

Some typesetters rectify both widows and orphans automatically. However, that's not as simple a process as it sounds. To avoid an orphan, we just move the entire line to the next page, which causes a single line space at the bottom of the page. To move a widow, we may have to move an entire line, which causes a space between paragraphs.

Some typesetters argue that in trying to fix a widow or orphan, the page might look untidier than it did before. So, whether to fix widows or orphans is either yours or the typesetter's call. I let my typesetter take that call.

#13 Word Stacks: When two consecutive rows of sentences start or end with the same letter or same word, it is not visually pleasing to the eye. So, typesetters try to ensure that two consecutive rows do not begin or end with the same word.

#14 Book Blocks: Book blocks are when blocks of text on pages facing each other end on the same row. Sometimes, we see that blocks of text on pages facing each other do not end on the same row. A visually pleasing image is when there is symmetry, and that is achieved when blocks of text end on the same row.

Do-it-Yourself or Hire a Professional?

Today, with the advent of several related software, it seems as though most authors can do the typesetting themselves, and some will be tempted. However, having personally experienced the problems this can cause if not done correctly, I have come to believe typesetting is a specialized job. Not everyone can do it well, and if you want your book to look professional, then I strongly suggest hiring a professional typesetter to do it for you. But I do understand that professionals can be expensive, and authors on a limited budget may want to have a go at doing it themselves.

To help you with this, I've listed some of the most popular software options for you to choose from.

MS Word: Can you typeset a book using Microsoft Word? Yes, it can be done. But, please, remember, MS Word was created to be a word processor and not a typesetting software. The result is, therefore, not going to be on a par with a professional grade; it's going to be average. Sometimes, average is acceptable to some people. If you're happy with that at this stage in your career as an author, then, yes, you can use MS Word to typeset your book.

Here's a basic step-by-step process to typesetting your book using MS Word:

1. To properly adjust the layout for your page, you'll first need to consider its **orientation,** margin, and size. You'll recall that I've already covered margin and size under the InDesign section. In this context, orientation simply means choosing between **landscape** or **portrait options,** the same ones we use when deciding the best way to photograph subjects on our devices. Landscape refers to a horizontal layout, while **portrait** refers to a vertical layout. Most books have a portrait layout.

2. Select the 'Layout' tab, which appears on the top menu bar of the Word document. Under 'Orientation,' 'Portrait' or 'Landscape' options will appear as a drop-down menu. Choose 'Portrait,' which is the standard form for most books.

   To set the **margins**, select the 'Layout' tab and click the 'Margins' command. Word comes with predefined margins, so opt for those, or set up your own custom margins. From the 'Layout' tab, click 'Margins', then click on **'Custom Margins'** and a page set up dialog box will appear. For a book sized 5.5x8.5", I recommend setting the following margins: Top 0.75", Bottom 0.75", Outside edge 0.75" (all three 19mm each). Set the margins, then click OK.

Lastly, you'll need to adjust the **page size.** The default size of 8x11" may be unsuitable for your project. So, if you need to change it, click 'Size' from the 'Layout' tab. Then select the appropriate size from the drop-down menu. A dialog box will appear. For a book of 5.5x8.5", set the width and height to 13.97cm x 12.59cm. Unfortunately, you cannot set up the **bleed** with Word, but you can set up slightly more space as previously discussed for the inside margin.

Adobe Indesign: The professionals use Indesign to design books. If you hire a professional typesetter, they will likely be using Indesign. If you want to do what the professionals do, then you should use Indesign too. Learning how to use the Indesign typesetting tools involves a bit of a learning curve, but if your desire to use it is strong, it can be mastered.

The following are the basic steps for typesetting a book using Adobe Indesign:

1. Set up a new document for your book. Click on **File > New > Document**

   Check **Facing pages**. Set the number of pages. Set the number of the starting page to 1 and set 'Intent to Print'.

   Select 'Custom' from the **Page Size** drop-down menu.

   Type **B-Format Paperback** into the textbox. The format is a standard industry size.

Set the **Width and Height** to reflect the size you want to model.

For example, take a book of size 6x9". This implies a width of 6 inches and a height of 9 inches. It is the **standard book size**. While one of 5.5x8.5" is a tad shorter and less in width too, it's vital to let you know that a 6x9" offers on average 20 percent more text space at an additional cost of about 5 percent in comparison to a 5.5"x8.5" size book. Note that width is the first value in the size.

Click **Add**

Click **OK**

Following all the steps above should have helped you to create a **Custom Page Size**, which you can save and reuse for other projects in the future.

2. Set the **Margins** and the **Bleeds**. Before you set both, I'll briefly explain what they mean. The margin refers to the edges of a page—the blank, rectangular portion surrounding the part of the page with text on it. As I've already said earlier in this chapter, margin sizing is something you need to be careful about because if you set them too small or too large, it could adversely affect readability.

As an example, for a book sized 5.5x8.5", I recommend using the following margin settings: Top 0.75", Bottom 0.75", Outside edge 0.75" (all three 19mm each), and Inside Binding edge 1.00" (25mm), and Page Bleed (each side) 0.125" (3.1mm).

You can think of the bleed as a portion of a printed page that provides a "margin of error." It's extra space that's added to the edge of the portion to be printed and which is later trimmed off. Say your page size is 11x8.5". You could add a bleed of 0.125". So, the page will need to be set at 11.25x8.75".

3. Click **OK**.

4. Set up **Masters**. Masters are the main lever and workhorse for smart typesetting. From **Pages**, InDesign inserts 'a Master' for you. It's the default that houses most of the body content. Right-click to rename it.

   When a text frame is placed within a Master, it will not be centered. Click **View,** then **Rulers** to drag the guide to the right 196mm and a second guide to the left 64mm.

5. Whatever dimensions you add to the Master will be automatically shown on all the pages which have the Master applied to them. To add beautiful **page numbering**, for example, scroll down to the bottom left of the page. From **Tools,** select **T** to create a small text frame. Set it at the center of the guide, with its top resting on the bottom margin. Choose the font you want and insert the kind of glyph you like.

   Select the 'Type Tool' and click the frame.

   Next, go to **Type > Insert Special Character > Markers > Current Page Number.**

   Set the **font** type, its **size**, and adjust its **orientation** to 'Center'. Set the **color** to black. You can easily do the above using the **Character Formatting Controls** at the top of the screen.

6. To add the page title and chapter headings, follow the process above. Instead of having the text frame below, it'll now be above. You'll paste the text frames onto the top of each page of the Master in the center.

7. Add the text frame for the main text of the book. Select the 'T' from 'Type tool' as before and create a text frame with a width and height suitable for the body content. Naturally, it'll be the largest frame. Its Y-axis will run from the left edge of the page to the right edge, and it'll start under the page title. Copy and paste it in a similar position on the second page. In the bottom right-hand corner of the first page, you'll see a tiny box; click on it, then click on the text frame on the next page to connect both frames together.

8. You'll need to create a second **Master** for pages where a chapter begins. Follow the process outlined above. Since it's for chapter beginnings, the text will start lower on the page than usual after the chapter heading.

9. Finally, insert the body content. First, ensure the Masters are applied to all pages. Select **Apply Master to Pages** from the 'Pages' drop-down menu. Then, copy and paste your content. The frame will be filled with text. At the bottom right corner, you'll see a small plus sign—it shows the content has overflowed its frame. Click on it and click on the next frame, and InDesign will automatically make the adjustment for you. From **Styles,** you can save the Masters for reuse on other books in the future.

Some authors have spent time on it and mastered typesetting. As I've mentioned, I personally don't do it for myself, preferring to use a professional typesetter to typeset my books. While it costs a little extra,

I find typesetting to be such a tricky and time-consuming process, I can find much better ways to spend that time!

If you are interested in hiring a professional typesetter, consider hiring my company, PublishEdge (visit www.publishedge.com), where we provide 'done-for-you' solutions. Authors can focus on writing while we take care of all the mundane aspects of self-publishing, like typesetting, editing, cover design, and distribution.

Chapter 4

Ebooks

The entire world is digital today. From booking a cab to ordering a pizza, we do almost everything on our mobile devices. Smartphones and tablets have revolutionized the world. Gone are the days when we had to wait in line at a bank to withdraw money. Even paper checks have been replaced by digital transfers of money. Having said that, why should books be left behind?

An ebook is a book in electronic format, so the 'e' stands for electronic. They are usually read with ereaders like Kindle, Nook, or Kobo, or you can read them by downloading the app onto your smartphone, computer, or tablet.

History of Ebooks

Amazon launched the ebook reader in the US in 2007, the same year Apple launched the iPhone. Two years later, Barnes and Noble came out with Nook. And 2010 saw the launch of Apple's iBooks and Google's eBookstore. By 2012, ebook revenues in the US were over $3 billion and surpassed hardcover sales.

Ebooks may have become popular in the last few decades, but the idea of an ereader can be traced to writer Bob Brown in the 1930s when he wrote an entire book titled *The Readies*.[23]

Brown wrote about his imagined ereader as, "A simple reading machine which I can carry or move around, attach to any old electric light plug and read hundred-thousand-word novels in ten minutes if I want to, and I want to."[24]

Today, ereaders have evolved into sleek machines which aim to imitate the print book experience. Ebooks can also be read via an app on your smartphone, tablet, or PC.

Why Ebooks?

Ebooks promise authors higher profits, largely because there are no associated printing costs, as with print publishing.

Yes, the biggest advantage of an ebook is that there are no printing costs when producing it. For example, a 200-page print book costs approximately $3.5 to print. If you price the book at $10, then the book's profit after deducting profit share with Amazon or other online retailers is just $2.50.

---

23   "The History of EBooks from 1930's 'Readies' to Today's GPO EBook Services," Government Book Talk, March 10, 2014, https://govbooktalk.gpo.gov/2014/03/10/the-history-of-ebooks-from-1930s-readies-to-todays-gpo-ebook-services/.

24   Jennifer Schuessler, "The Godfather of the E-Reader," The New York Times (The New York Times, April 8, 2010), https://www.nytimes.com/2010/04/11/books/review/Schuessler-t.html.

On the other hand, an ebook priced at $4.99 with a 70 percent profit share with Amazon yields a higher profit for the author. Even when pricing the ebook at half the print book price, you still make a higher profit.

Instant Download

Ebook readers don't have to wait for their books to be shipped or worry about missing a delivery. They can download and read any book they want almost instantly.

Convenience

Today, I can carry thousands of ebooks on my smartphone. If I am waiting for someone at the café, train station, or outside someone's office, I can pull out my smartphone and choose from any number of ebooks to read. Ereaders and smartphones are portable and fit in my pocket, whereas I obviously cannot carry a paperback in my pocket!

Searchable

The search feature in an ebook is a great draw. If readers forget something, they can use the search function to find it within the book. Of course, this isn't ever an option with any print book. If you haven't noted it down, it's a case of flipping through the pages until you find what you're looking for.

Increase Font Size

If the font size of an ebook is too small for comfortable reading, most ereaders allow the user to increase it. Sometimes, we want to increase font sizes to read more easily, and it's a great option to have for readers who find some font sizes too small.

Bookmarks

Many ereaders also allow you to place electronic bookmarks. It's a handy feature because you can start where you left off or come back to something later.

Technology has made ereaders a popular choice among readers. They have evolved rapidly in the last decade and are now competing with physical books for readers' attention.

Authors can also write fewer words and more topic-focused ebooks that take far less turnaround time to produce than traditional print books.

You might ask if you should publish a print book or an ebook. I would say, why not do both? Nowadays, it's easy to convert a print book into an ebook and make it available on ebook platforms. Ebooks provide authors with an additional revenue stream alongside paperback sales. Authors and readers benefit when writers create ebooks as well as paperback versions of their books. For writers, it's a great way to open your work up to a whole new market of ereaders, and readers can take advantage of the options and features of ebooks.

File Formats of Ebooks

The two most common ebook file formats are Mobi and EPUB. There are other formats, too, including AZW, IBA, LRX, FB2, DJVU, LIT, and RFT.

If you're planning to self-publish, the only format you need to concern yourself with is EPUB.

It is the most widely used format and should work on most platforms.

I generally prefer formatting my files in EPUB because it works on most ebook platforms. However, it's worth noting that if you're publishing your ebook on Amazon alone, then you'll find yourself using Mobi, which is Amazon's preferred ebook format. But Amazon accepts EPUB files as well. So if you format your ebook in EPUB, you should be fine on most platforms.

Ebooks can be formatted in either a 'flow-through' or 'fixed' format.

A flow-through format means the ebook adjusts for reading according to the device, so the book could look different if you read it on, say, a notepad as compared to a smartphone.

With a fixed format, the ebook does not adjust according to the device, and the formatting looks the same on every device.

Ideally, it's best if ebooks have a flow-through or reflowable format because it will then fit into any screen irrespective of the device it's being viewed on. The only exception is if you have too many pictures in your ebook.

How to Format an Ebook?

You have two options here: Do it yourself, or get it done through a professional. I usually get the formatting done by a professional, although there are authors who do it themselves. To do it yourself properly, you need to have or develop an understanding of either of the software packages listed below. That means going through the learning curve of using them effectively, which could be time-consuming.

- Vellum
- Indesign
- Scrivener

Other options for formatting your ebook besides these software packages are KindleCreate by Amazon and Draft2Digital, another self-publishing platform that helps you format your ebook.

Next, I'll briefly explain the processes involved in using some of these software packages to format your ebook.

How to Use Scrivener to Format an Ebook?

We'll cover three simple phases. They include:

- Setting up your chapters
- Laying out your front matter
- Compiling your ebook

Chapters are known as 'folders' in Scrivener. So, set up each chapter in your ebook as a separate folder in Scrivener, and give each one the title you've chosen (and number them if you wish). Label and lay out each chapter precisely the way you want it to appear in the ebook. If you've used Scrivener to write the book in the first place, you'll only need to clean the text up a bit before you compile the ebook. You should also treat the back matter similarly. That is to say, it should be an individual folder.

On the left-hand side of the screen, below 'Chapters', you'll find 'Front matter'. Your prologue, title page, dedication, and copyright page are usually what make up the front matter. Add each part of the front matter content. You'll also need to add your cover page. And what about the TOC (Table of Contents)? Scrivener automatically generates that for you.

After you've completed the steps above, click on the 'File' menu located near the 'Format as' menu. You'll be presented with a window in the middle or to the right of the page showing 'Contents'. Click on 'Format as' and select 'Original'. Then, at the bottom, you'll see 'Compile for'. Click on the drop-down menu and select 'Kindle (Mobi)'.

At the bottom, you'll see 'Add front matter'. Select it, and then select 'Ebook'. This will ensure that your front matter is included in the compiled file. Then, in the middle or right-hand part of the screen, a window will open and present you with a list of all the content you want to compile. Make sure each item of content you want to be compiled shows 'Include' next to it.

Click on 'Cover' and on the cover image you will have already uploaded.

Click on 'Formatting' to edit chapter titles if needed. Also, check the 'Transformations, References, and Footnotes' tab if either are relevant. In the section for 'Metadata', include the copyright statement, author name, book title, and add your ISBN as your 'Custom unique identifier'.

For KindleGen. You'll need this link:

https://www.amazon.com/gp/feature. html?ie=UTF8&docId=1000765211 to convert your book to the Mobi format. On the page, you'll find Amazon's stance on the Mobi format—its use is no longer encouraged. EPUB is now preferred. But if you are using Mobi, download the software, extract it, and direct Scrivener to where you have saved it; Scrivener will then install it. You'll need the link above to access Kindle Previewer 3 to check your Mobi files.

Use 'Save Preset' and it will save all the settings for your book. Click on the 'Compile' button and wait. And that's it—you'll have your ebook in Mobi format. If it's EPUB you prefer, then select 'EPUB book' from the 'Compile for' menu, click the 'Compile' button, and you're done!

How to Use Draft2Digital to Format an Ebook?

Draft2Digital is a much more automated system—it does most of the work for you.

You'll need your chapter headings to appear larger and bolder than the rest of the text if you want Draft2Digital to recognize them. Ideally, use H1 for them. Use heading styles only for material you want to appear in the TOC.

To differentiate the font size of chapter headings to the main text, simply scale up by adding four points. So, if the regular text is twelve points, use sixteen points for the heading text. However, be warned, Draft2Digital uses a default serif font that cannot be changed. Plus, all the lines are automatically set to a single space and cannot be changed. But you can use three empty lines to insert scene breaks. Draft2Digital will automatically create your front and back matter for you.

For any relevant images you have in Word, *don't* copy and paste them. Instead, make sure they're embedded in the document, then simply use the insert function.

How to Use KindleCreate to Format an Ebook?

KindleCreate (KC) is simple and straightforward to use. It's definitely what I'd choose if I were a beginner. Let's see how it works.

Download KC and install it. Then, import your manuscript into it. To do this, start KC and click on 'Create new'. Find the file of your manuscript. KC will automatically find and format the chapter titles. Check that the chapters KC finds are correct. Then, click on '**Accept Selected**'.

KC displays your book in three facets: Front Matter, Body, and Back Matter. It's straightforward to add front matter. Say you'd like to add the title page; first click on the + sign next to the 'Front Matter' section and select the title page. For example, if it's the copyright page, click the + sign and select 'Copyright Page'. The formatted pages will then be automatically generated for you. That's it.

What about the TOC? KC automatically updates it for you. That's to say, when you add or remove material, it reflects the changes. But how do you set it up in the first place? This is how to do it: Click on your first chapter in the 'Contents panel', click 'Insert' and choose 'Table of Contents'. A list of detected chapter titles will then be displayed.

Check what's shown and if it's correct, then click OK, and the TOC will be added. It'll also help you style your titles. And, if you'd like to apply drop caps and spacing between the title and the first paragraph, simply click next to the first word on the page, then go to the 'Text Properties' pane and click the 'Chapter First Paragraph' button.

There's a default theme that comes with KC, but you can update your book with other themes. To insert an image, right-click where you'd like to insert it, click 'Insert Image'. Then, find the image on your computer and open it. The image is inserted for you. If you'd like to insert hyperlinks, first highlight the word to be linked, right-click on it, and then click 'Insert Hyperlink'. Enter the relevant URL in the box and click 'Insert Hyperlink'.

To control the headers and footers, click 'Print Settings'. Preview the file and click 'Publish' on the upper right-hand corner of KC, and a KPF file will be ready for you to upload to KDP.

How to Use Vellum to Format an Ebook?

Vellum is currently available for Mac users only, but it's very simple to use. You can start with a trial version. The first thing to do is to import your manuscript into Vellum. It accepts all documents with a .docx extension. Alternatively, you can create a new project in Vellum and then copy and paste your manuscript. To do this, click 'File', then 'New'.

Vellum's interface has three facets: right, center, and left. The left side is the navigator; that's where you can access and organize the content and formatting styles of your manuscript. The center is your workspace; that's where you make changes, while the right side is where you preview any changes you've made.

After you've imported your manuscript, Vellum will prompt you to enter author info, title, and subtitle. Select the 'Ebook Cover' tab at the top of the page to easily upload your ebook. During the import, Vellum auto-recognizes your chapters, but always remember to check the navigator to ensure it's been done correctly.

If you'd prefer to split your chapters yourself, first click on your manuscript in the navigator. In the panel in the middle, place your cursor before the start of a new chapter in the text, then select 'Chapter' and select 'Split chapter'. To view files at the center, select them in the navigator. Vellum also generates your TOC for you. To add a new chapter, select 'Chapter', then 'Add' your chapter. To add an element of the book that's not a chapter, simply select 'Element, then 'Add' the element. At the top of the navigator, you'll find styles, which you can use to change the styles in your ebook.

Check the navigator to ensure that your files are arranged the way you'd like them to appear in your ebook. If you need to rearrange them, simply click and drag them to the appropriate location.

The right panel allows you to preview your ebook as it'll appear in Kindle Fire. To see how it'll be displayed in other formats, select the phone icon and choose your preference. Once you're happy, click on 'Generate', and your ebook is ready!

If you are good with software and willing to spend time rather than money, then doing it yourself might be an option for you. But if you do not want the inconvenience of formatting your ebook, you can hire an agency to do it for you. Although they'll charge a small fee, it can save you a lot of time.

There's no doubt that ebooks are here to stay. Paperback files can easily be converted to ebooks, and they provide a great opportunity for authors to serve an online audience. So, seeing how easy it is to self-publish using today's selection of dedicated software, it almost goes without saying that you should have your book published in an electronic format!

Chapter 5

Audiobook Production

Do you know that, in 2019, the revenues generated from the sales of audiobooks in the US were more than the revenue from ebook sales?[25] This statistic clearly shows why the rapidly growing demand for audiobooks can potentially be a good source of revenue for authors.

What Is an Audiobook and How Does It Work?

Many readers will already know what an audiobook is and probably enjoy listening to them. However, for those still unaware of the phenomenon, let me explain a little about how it works. An audiobook is simply a digital audio file where the author or a narrator narrates an entire book for the listener's enjoyment. Listeners purchase their choice of an audiobook, of which there are literally thousands to choose from, from a growing number of online audiobook producers. Two of the earliest to capitalize on this market and, therefore, the largest and most popular are Amazon's Audible and Audiobooks.com. The audiobook retailer provides a free app that listeners can install on their device, so they can

---

25 Michael Kozlowski, "Audiobook Trends and Statistics for 2020," Reader (Good e-Reader, June 21, 2020), https://goodereader.com/blog/audiobooks/audiobook-trends-and-statistics-for-2020.

then simply download the audiobook onto the app and listen to it at their convenience. The process works in a very similar way to a Kindle app. For authors, the beauty of an audiobook is that it attracts an audience that includes people who are not generally vociferous readers of print or ebooks but nevertheless enjoy listening to a book of their choice. Producing an audio version of your book opens it up to this growing new non-reading audience. Listeners can access the audiobook via their device easily anywhere and listen to it at their leisure, maybe on the long commute home from work, before bed, or even while taking a shower!

Another advantage of audiobooks for authors is that they are priced higher than ebooks. Plus, there are many readers of ebooks and print books who also enjoy listening to audiobooks. So, looking at this growing phenomenon overall, audiobooks present authors with a great opportunity to tap into another kind of audience that may not otherwise know about or have read your book.

Is *Your* Book Suitable to Be Made into an Audiobook?

Not all books are suited to the audiobook format. For instance, if your book contains too many images, statistics, tables, or other technical stuff, it probably won't suit the format. However, if your content is mostly text, and you've made the effort to tell a great story engagingly, it's likely your book will be well suited to become an audiobook. But, how do you go about producing an audiobook?

The first step, of course, is to complete writing and editing your manuscript. Your manuscript should be of a ready-to-publish quality. Then, you need to make a few important decisions: Are you going to narrate the manuscript yourself? Or will you get a professional voice-over artist to narrate it for you? I've heard some people recommend that authors narrate their book themselves, but I disagree with that.

In my experience, most authors who do their own narration, even the bestselling ones, don't do such a great job. To be sure of the appeal of your book to audiences, I recommend hiring a professional voice-over artist well versed in working on audiobooks to handle the narration and production of the book for you. There's a good reason for this: Narrating and producing an audiobook takes a substantial investment of time and energy. Approximately 9,400 words of text equals one hour of audio content. It can take anywhere from two to three hours to record one hour of finished content. It can take another three hours to edit that content. Initially, when I started to record my content, it took way more than three hours to record one hour of content. That was because I'm not a professional, and I was doing it for the first time. In short, it takes at least six hours to produce one hour of an audiobook. So, that is thirty-six hours of labor to finish recording and editing a 60,000-word book.

In addition to this, there's a steep learning curve involved, demanding even more time. The time it takes to produce an audiobook and the learning curve you face if you do it yourself are two big reasons why I choose not to narrate my own audiobooks. Instead, I hire a professional voice-over artist to do it for me. I'd rather use that time to write rather than narrate. So, by hiring a professional, I not only save time, but I can also be confident that the production quality of the audiobook will be of a high standard. I strongly recommend that all authors do the same. Yes, hiring a professional costs me money, but I don't mind paying for good quality.

I think the only exception to this is if the author in question is a professional voice-over artist themselves and has extensive audio production expertise, which seems highly unlikely. My company can produce and distribute audiobooks for you. Just visit our website https://www.publishedge.com/solutions/

There are two ways to produce an audiobook. You can produce your audiobook on Amazon's Audible or through an audiobook distributor like Findaway Voices.com.[26] You can either hire an audio production company or service provider who can create the audio files for you, and you can upload them yourself onto either Audible or Findaway Voices. Once you've uploaded the files, there's a wait, as both platforms take several weeks to approve them. Once the files are approved, Findaway Voices will distribute your audiobook to several audiobook retailers for you, including Amazon's Audible.

You can also find a voice-over artist on both Findaway Voices and Audible. You can pay them a fixed fee, which is generally at least $250 per finished hour (approximately 9,400 words equals one finished hour). Or, if you want to save money or cannot afford to pay that much, it's possible to do a revenue share deal with your narrator. That means you agree that they will keep a certain percentage of the revenues from the audiobook sales in payment. It's entirely your call on which model suits you best. I prefer to pay a fixed fee, and I haven't yet done a revenue share with a narrator, but the opportunity is there.

Numbering Files

File names should begin with a three-digit number that indicates the order of appearance of the files. For example: 000_opening_credits. mp3, 001_title.mp3, 002_title.mp3, 003_title.mp3.

The format of the files should be mp3 or higher, and your voice-over artist or production company should provide you with the files in the correct format.

---

26   "Create and Sell Audiobooks," Findaway Voices, accessed August 29, 2021, https://findawayvoices.com/.

The files should include opening credits, closing credits, and a retail sample. The retail sample is a short sample from the book, which is generally one to five minutes long.

Opening credits include:

```
[title of audiobook]
Written by [name of author]
Narrated by [name of narrator]
```

Closing credits include:

```
Written by [name of author]
Narrated by [name of narrator]
Copyright [year and name of copyright holder]

Produced by [Company name]
```

Before closing this chapter, I'd like to quote once more the statistic I opened with. In 2019, the revenues generated from the sales of audiobooks in the US totaled more than that from ebooks.[27] There's no doubt, then, that audiobooks are here to stay and present authors with a rapidly growing alternative marketplace for selling their books. If you have the budget or are willing to make a revenue share deal with an equally willing voice-over artist, I strongly recommend making the move and converting your ebook into an audiobook. It'll give you access to a whole new audience that maybe doesn't have the time or inclination to read print and ebooks but still enjoys listening to a good book. When you look at all the many benefits of going audible, you can see why I'm a big fan of audiobooks. The cost of producing an audiobook might be slightly higher than for an ebook, but it can provide authors with a healthy additional revenue stream which deserves exploration.

---

27   Michael Kozlowski, "Audiobook Trends and Statistics for 2020," Reader.

Chapter 6

Distribution Channels

Book distribution is the act of making your book available in bookstores, online retailers, or any other book purchasing channel.

It makes sense that the potential for sales of your book increases if it is available in the most popular places where readers buy books.

Let's explore some of the most popular distribution channels.

'Bricks and Mortar' Bookstores

Although the number of bricks and mortar bookstores has fallen dramatically in the last two decades, they still exist. Statistics experts Statista predicted a figure of 22.6 thousand in the US alone for 2018.[28] Moreover, bookstore sales revenue in the US was $10.28 billion in 2018.[29] Also, in 2019, Barnes & Noble, one of the largest bookstores in the US,

---

28 Amy Watson, "Number of Bookstores in the U.S. 2017," Statista, June 15, 2013, https://www.statista.com/statistics/249027/number-of-bookstores-in-the-us/.

29 Ibid.

netted $3.48 billion in sales. Such a vast market cannot be discounted when thinking of distributing your book for sale.

Let's also remember that many neighborhoods have their own smaller, independent book shops and are usually home to a few big chain stores that don't just sell books but also music and gadgets, a variety of goods that attract customers who might also decide to buy a book.

Barnes & Noble is one of the larger chain bookstores in the US, but there are others, including Bookmans, Books-A-Million, and Powell's Books.

The UK also has its big book retailer stores on the high street, including W H Smith, Waterstones, The Works, and Foyles.

Landmark, Crossword Bookstores, Oxford Bookstore, and Sapna Book House are popular among the big chains in India.

Bookstores mostly buy from wholesalers, although some smaller bookshops sometimes buy directly from the author or publisher.

If you're a self-published author who wants to get their book in front of a bigger audience, it's worth approaching the management of your local bookstore to see if you can make a deal where they would sell your book in return for you marketing the store to your audience. Most independent stores are happy to promote local authors.

You might also be able to provide a bigger margin to your local bookshop than a wholesaler since they are buying directly from you as opposed to a distributor. To do this, you'll have to get your books printed by, say, a local printer and stock them at your local bookshop. Of course, this involves some financial investment in printing and marketing, but you could profit from the arrangement if your book sells well.

Direct Sales

As an author, there are several tried and trusted ways for you to sell your book. You can do it directly from your own website, via a toll-free number, by door-to-door selling, or at conferences, fairs, and similar events.

Although the direct sales method is time-consuming, it can be a great way to build an author's visibility, for instance, through launch events, workshops, and seminars.

Libraries

With more than 100,000 libraries in the US alone, libraries present a massive opportunity for book sales. If you sell just one copy of your book to each of these libraries, that is 100,000 copies. Even if you only manage to sell to just 10 percent, that is still 10,000 books, which is not bad at all!

Online Retailers

Amazon is the largest and most popular online retailer of books in the world. More books are sold on Amazon than through any other online retailer. Self-published authors can sell both print and ebooks from Amazon.

Although most book sales happen on Amazon, there are thousands of other online retailers out there who sell books.

The major brick-and-mortar retailers like Powell's Books, Books-A-Million, and Barnes & Noble also sell books through their online portals.

Some of the other popular online retailers of books are Alibris, Peachpit, Better World Books, Booktopia, Biblio, and The Book People.

Since most online retailers are print-on-demand, it's unlikely you'll need to maintain an inventory.

Making Your Book Available on Each of These Online Retailers

There are two ways to make your book available for sale. You can either set up an account and upload your files directly with each of these online retailers, or you can use an aggregator.

If you set up your account with an aggregator, it will distribute your books to thousands of retailers in its network.

The advantage of using an aggregator is that you need to only maintain one account. Aggregators make money by taking a percentage out of every sale.

Whereas if you set up an account directly with hundreds of online retailers, you'd need to open an account with each of them and then go through an approval process with them all individually. You can imagine how time-consuming and impractical that would be!

Some authors focus on the largest online retailers and ignore the rest.

Aggregators

The biggest advantage of an aggregator is that you only need to maintain one account. Amazon might represent more than 80 percent of the book market, and a few other big players along with Amazon might comprise 90 percent of the market, but some authors prefer to go with an aggregator so their book has a much wider distribution span.

Let's look at some of the most popular aggregators for print books.

Amazon Expanded Distribution

Amazon is a retailer, but it also provides aggregation services through which it makes your book available to other retailers, bookstores, and libraries.

All you need to do when you sign up is check the box that says "Expanded Distribution." By checking that box, Amazon will make your book available to its network of distributors, retailers, and libraries.

Note, however, that if a book sells through Amazon's network, the royalty share is 60 percent. If the sale happens through its expanded network, then the royalty is 40 percent.

Royalties are calculated as (royalty rate x list price) minus printing costs = royalty. For example, if your book retails at $20 and the printing costs are $4, then your royalty is 40% x $20 minus $4, which is $4.

Kindle Direct Publishing's (KDP) royalties are slightly less than IngramSpark's. Please note, if you choose KDP expanded distribution and try to upload your book on IngramSpark as well, it will create a conflict. If you plan on publishing your book on both KDP and IngramSpark, then make sure *not* to choose KDP's expanded distribution option.

Pros

There's a higher royalty rate if you choose Amazon's 'Standard Distribution' option rather than expanded distribution as author royalties for Amazon's standard distribution are 60 percent.

Another benefit for authors is that their book becomes available for sale on the Amazon website very quickly.

Amazon takes about 72 hours to approve your manuscript and book cover. Once Amazon approves your files, your book will be available for purchase on Amazon's website almost immediately.

Cons

As just mentioned, there's a lower royalty rate for choosing Amazon's expanded distribution option.

The royalty rate for Amazon's expanded distribution is 40 percent, so profits get eaten up by lower royalties.

There are no printing facilities in countries like India, so buyers from the second largest internet market may have to pay for overseas shipping.

Amazon only offers the paperback format and not hardcover.

IngramSpark

IngramSpark is one of the largest distributors of print and ebooks in the US. It has its own printing facilities and several print-on-demand partners across the world.

IngramSpark helps with the distribution of paperback, hardcover, and ebooks.

IngramSpark can be a better choice than KDP's expanded distribution, depending on your goals. The royalty rate for IngramSpark is better than KDP's expanded distribution. Plus, your book will be distributed to libraries, academic institutions, and over 39,000 retailers all over the world, including Amazon, Barnes & Noble, Kobo, Apple, Walmart, and many others. But their printing costs seem to be slightly higher than Amazon's.

One of the biggest advantages of IngramSpark is its global Connect Program, which allows any book it sells to be printed by its partners in India, Germany, Spain, Russia, China, South Korea, and other countries.

IngramSpark has a much broader distribution network than Amazon's KDP.

IngramSpark does not call the profits from book sales royalties; instead, it calls them a 'distributor discount.' The concept is the same, but the name is different. For example, a 40 percent distributor discount means you are discounting your book by 40 percent for the distributor; that essentially means a royalty of 60 percent.

With IngramSpark, you have the opportunity to discount your book anywhere between 35 percent to 55 percent. The higher the discount, the more lucrative it becomes for the distributor.

Traditional distributors can buy the book at a 55 percent discount, distribute it to bookstores at a lower discount, and keep a certain percentage as their profit. Another decision you'll need to make is if your book should be returnable or unreturnable. What does unreturnable mean? It means that if bookstores don't sell your book, they can return it for a refund.

Discounting your book at 55 percent and making your book returnable is your best chance of getting it into bookstores. The discount makes your book an attractive prospect for bookstores and distributors. They make the highest profit with a 55 percent discount, and if your book doesn't sell, they can return it. It has zero risks for the distributor and the bookstore. But you, as the author-publisher, are taking the highest risk.

So, should you discount your book by 55 percent and make it returnable?

It depends on your marketing strategy. If most people are buying books from your mailing list, it makes sense to offer the least discount of 35 percent because it offers the highest profit for you.

Most distributors and bookstores will not necessarily be doing the marketing for you. If you discount your books by 55 percent, you may have to price your books higher or cut costs on your marketing.

There's a balance involved. For example, some people might discount their books at 35 percent, but they keep their book pricing low and spend more money on marketing. Others spend less on marketing but discount their books to the maximum possible extent.

Clearly, discounting is a tricky call and one that every self-published author needs to make based on their individual marketing strategy.

IngramSpark has one small disadvantage when compared to Amazon's expanded distribution, though; when you order author copies, the cost is slightly higher.

Another disadvantage with IngramSpark is that it charges a small fee to publish with the company. Having said that, many independent authors don't mind paying the fee because it saves them time and gives them access to a much wider distribution network.

Your book can take up to two weeks to appear on Amazon's website.

A good option could be to set up on Amazon's standard distribution, uncheck the expanded distribution option, and simultaneously set up on IngramSpark. Please note, if you set up on Amazon's expanded distribution, you won't be able to set up on IngramSpark, so you must uncheck the expanded distribution box on Amazon to be able to publish on IngramSpark too.

Lulu

Lulu offers another distribution option if you don't want to use Amazon's expanded distribution or IngramSpark. Lulu has fairly good reviews from authors. Like IngramSpark, Lulu also distributes to some of the largest online retailers.

The only reason I can see why authors use Lulu over the other two is because, as I mentioned in the chapter on ebooks, Lulu offers book sizes that are not available with other aggregators.

As you already know, I encourage authors to stick to standard book sizes of 5x8", 5.5x8.5", or 6x9". Personally, I prefer sticking to one book size for all my books because when I stack them on a bookshelf, they look neat and uniform.

Both Amazon expanded distribution and IngramSpark have the option to publish with the three book sizes mentioned above. Lulu has all the same options except the 5x8". So, if your book is typeset to 5x8", then you must change the size for it to be accepted on Lulu.

Amazon Expanded Distribution, IngramSpark, and Lulu are the most popular self-publishing options for both print and ebooks.

Wide Versus Exclusive to Amazon

There are also some authors who are exclusive to Amazon (Kindle Direct Publishing (KDP)).

Being exclusive to Amazon means that your book is available only on Amazon and no other online retailer.

Amazon does offer certain benefits to authors in return for this exclusivity. Amazon's exclusivity program is called KDP Select.

With KDP Select, readers who subscribe to Kindle Unlimited can access your ebook for free, and you get paid a certain share of their subscription via the KDP Select Global Fund, depending on the number of pages they read from your ebook—*but only for the first time they read them.*

Once you enroll in Kindle Select, you are automatically enrolled in the Kindle Lending Library program, where Amazon Prime customers get to read one book a month for free.

You can also run a promotion where you offer your readers a free download of your ebook for five days in a ninety-day period.

Another feature of KDP Select is that you can also participate in Kindle Countdown Deals, which are time-limited reader discounts or free offers.[30]

In summary, the benefits of being exclusive to Amazon include being enrolled in Kindle Unlimited and Kindle Lending Library programs, free

---

30 "Royalties in Kindle Unlimited," Kindle Direct Publishing, accessed August 29, 2021, https://kdp.amazon.com/en_US/help/topic/G201541130.

promotion for five days in a ninety-day period, and the option to use Kindle Countdown Deals.

So, should you choose KDP Select and be exclusive to Amazon?

Let's evaluate the pros and the cons.

Amazon is one of the largest online retailers of books in the world. Many people have found it beneficial to be exclusive to Amazon because they only need to focus on one platform. There is a time-consuming learning curve involved in mastering each platform individually. Besides, with the entire sales and reporting consolidated to one place, administrative work is significantly reduced.

The promotion benefits of Amazon that include Kindle Unlimited, Kindle Lending Library program, Countdown Deals, and free promotion for five days in a ninety-day period can give you visibility and help you gain loyal readers who will eventually buy your future books and training programs.

There is one disadvantage with KDP Select.

The obvious disadvantage of going exclusive with Amazon is that you are missing out on the thousands of other distribution channels. The opportunity to 'go wide' on your distribution is lost.

Other than losing out on going wide, I don't see any other disadvantage with being exclusive to Amazon.

My personal preference has been to go wide. I rarely sign up to go exclusive with Amazon. I may have to buy my own ISBN rather than use Amazon's free ISBN, but that's the price authors must pay to go wide with their distribution.

Ebook Distribution

There are also several aggregators exclusively for ebooks, and I cover the most widely used below.

Draft2Digital

Draft2Digital only distributes ebooks. They distribute to Barnes & Noble, Kobo, iBooks, Scribd, Inktera, Tolino, 24Symbols, Playster, and many more. If you set up with IngramSpark, they distribute to the bigger ebook players like Barnes & Noble, Kobo, and iBooks as well. With Draft2Digital, along with the bigger ebook retailers, you get the chance to distribute to some of the off-beat distribution channels as well.

Besides, Draft2Digital also helps you format your ebook for free. At the time of writing, Draft2Digital is exploring distributing paperbacks as well.

Smashwords

After Amazon's KDP, Smashwords is the next best option for distributing your eBooks. Although Amazon's KDP gives authors a 70 percent royalty on sales of ebooks, Smashwords gives 85 percent of royalties on ebooks sold on the Smashwords store. As an aggregator, Smashwords distributes your ebook to several platforms globally. Their royalty rates vary for books sold on other platforms through their distribution network.

Smashwords distribution network includes Apple Books, Kobo, Barnes & Noble, Baker & Taylor, Scribd, OverDrive (which serves over 20,000 libraries), Gardners, Odilio, and many more.

Smashwords has been around a lot longer than Draft2Digital and carries far more industry clout than Draft2Digital.

Besides Draft2Digital and Smashwords, there are other off-beat options like Gumroad, Unbound, and Inkshares.

Finally, the decision whether you want to go direct, use one aggregator, or use multiple aggregators is a matter of choice. It depends greatly on your personal situation. Some people may not like a particular user interface or reporting mechanism and might choose one option over the other purely for irrational reasons.

Personally, I like to have fewer distractions to focus on and instead spend most of my time writing rather than on administrative tasks.

Audiobook Distribution

There are two ways to distribute your audiobook. One is by creating an account with every single audiobook retailer. The other is to find an aggregator which will distribute your book to all those retailers. The advantage of an aggregator is that you only need to upload your book on the aggregator's platform, and it will distribute your audiobook to several retailers. The sales and revenue reports are also consolidated, and you only need to upload your book and access reports using a single platform. The disadvantage is that the aggregator will take a small share from the book sales as their fee.

The Top Audiobook Retailers

Audible (ww.acx.com) – ACX has both exclusive and nonexclusive agreements. If you are exclusive to ACX, you cannot publish your book anywhere else. ACX distributes to Audible, Amazon, and iTunes. Your audiobook will be limited to these three retailers if you choose to be exclusive to ACX. The advantage of exclusivity is that you have a higher royalty share compared to being non-exclusive. However, ACX does not accept authors from all countries. So, if you are based outside the US, check to see if Audible accepts authors from your country. If it doesn't accept authors from your country, the next best option is to use an aggregator which distributes to Audible. Also, Audible doesn't allow authors to choose their pricing; Audible chooses the pricing for you, which is something to keep in mind. You can upload your book onto Audible by visiting   https://www.acx.com/help/audio-publishers/200679720.   You first create an account and then upload your book onto Audible.

Audible currently holds the majority of the audiobook market. Most audiobook listeners use Audible to listen to their audiobooks. So, it makes sense to be on the biggest market.

Other than Audible, other top audiobook retailers include:

- Nook Audiobooks
- Apple
- Google Play
- Audiobooks.com

Once you have your files ready, you can sign up and upload your files onto the platforms of your chosen audiobook retailer(s).

Instead of publishing via each of these retailers separately, you can upload onto one aggregator platform, which will distribute your book to most of these retailers.

To help, I've listed some of the top aggregators of audiobooks below.

Findaway Voices (FV) is a one-stop solution for creating, distributing, and earning money from audiobooks. FV will help distribute your ebook to over forty retailers and even provide sales support. They take 20 percent of sales, while you keep 80 percent.

Authors Republic distributes your audiobooks to over fifty retailers. You keep 70 percent of sales, while they take 30 percent. AR is a 'pure aggregator.' That means, unlike FV, it doesn't engage in content creation. You have to plan, record, and package your audiobook yourself and then send AR the finished product. But it has a wider reach than FV and provides you with a dashboard from which you can monitor your audiobook's performance.

Scribl is a platform developed by authors who know all the pain points! Scribl helps you automate the process of reaching your audience. You get to keep 70 percent to 85 percent of sales, and you get paid within forty-eight hours. All the audiobooks on Scribl are packaged with free ebooks, making the offer more appealing to buyers.

It has a proprietary Story Elements System that automatically subdivides the books on the site into sub-genres as more and more books are uploaded. This helps authors generate more sales, as it brings a specificity that helps readers pinpoint exactly the kind of books they want.

Feiyr helps you distribute your ebooks to over 185 retailers. You keep 80 percent of your revenue. You'll only need to pay less than a $10 activation fee and less than a $10 publication fee for print-on-demand. There are no registration, annual, or monthly fees to pay.

Most aggregators are similar and distribute to similar retailers. If you have multiple audiobooks, you can experiment with different platforms and see which one works best for you.

Chapter 7

Pricing

Most self-published authors randomly price a book. Some of them are priced too low and others much too high. If you price your book too low, you're basically selling yourself short. Too high, and you risk readers not purchasing your book at all. That's why I recommend using a strategic and methodical approach when pricing your book, which I'm going to talk about now.

Here are some of the biggest mistakes made by self-published authors:

Pricing the Book Too Low

What's wrong with pricing a book too low?

Potentially low profits—ROI on marketing might not justify the low price. Profits could be unacceptably low. In fact, the spending on marketing and advertising might be much higher than the royalties from the book sales. In short, you might lose money on sales of the book as they may not justify the marketing spend.

Perceived value—Most people value a product based on the price. If you price your product too low, people may perceive your product to be inferior. So, that's another reason you don't want to price your product too low.

Pricing the Book Too High

Obviously, the opposite of pricing too low is pricing your book too high. Pricing your product too high is also a major problem because authors can effectively price themselves out of the market. For example, a client of mine priced his 120-page self-help ebook and paperback at $39.99. Although the author is a bestseller, that was a price readers were not used to paying. So, sales went down. Ideally, you want pricing to attract the maximum number of buyers *and* make yourself a decent profit.

There are four factors that affect pricing:

1. Genre
2. Length of the book
3. Credibility of the author
4. Goals of the author

The price range for a self-help book is quite different from that of, say, a romance novel, as you'll see from simply observing online bookstores. Readers expect to pay more or less, depending on the type and genre of book they're buying. Each type has its own pricing average. To find out the right pricing for your book, you'll first need to do some research on your genre to identify the general pricing range.

Let's take my book, *How to Write Your First Nonfiction Book,* and show you how I came up with the pricing for it.

I first went to Amazon and checked the category 'Authorship' because that's the category my book fits into best. This produced a list of bestsellers. I wasn't about to analyze the price of every bestseller listed;

I only looked at the books which closely resembled mine in terms of length and topic. My book is about 150 pages, so I looked for books of between 100 to 180 pages whose topic closely resembled mine. If you scroll down on the product page on Amazon, you'll see the book-length for each book.

The Art of Writing Well has about 109 pages, is priced at $4.99 for the ebook and $16.24 for the paperback.

Lifelong Writing Habit is about 104 pages, is priced at $2.99 for the ebook, and $8.99 for the paperback.

How to Write Nonfiction by Joseph Robinson is 168 pages, is priced at $2.99 for the ebook, and $19.87 for the paperback.

Dear Writer, Are You in Writer's Block? by Becca Syme is 114 pages, is priced at $4.99 for the ebook and $9.99 for the paperback.

I think these bestsellers are close enough in length and similar in topic to my book. I can safely conclude that the ebook price of $2.99–$4.99 is a price that readers are accustomed to paying for this type and length of the book. But the paperback pricing seems to be all over the place, ranging from $8.99 to $19.87. I didn't want to price my book at $19.87 because I want it to be affordable to most readers. At $12.95, my paperback pricing seems to be in the mid-range, neither too high nor too low. Once I get enough performance data on my Amazon ads, I will be able to tell if this pricing is optimum for my book. The good thing about pricing is that the price of the book can be changed as and when you prefer. You can start low and move upwards, or start high and move downwards. I like to start low and move upwards because I don't want to penalize early adopters. People who buy the book soonest should pay a lower price, while late adopters should pay slightly more. So, I believe it's best to make a lower start and move the price upwards based on the popularity of the book.

You can easily see from your stats whether book sales improve or reduce based on changes in price.

Goals of the Author

Sometimes, nonfiction authors want to give away books for free or for a low price because their main goal is to build their authority. Others want to build reviews. There are even others who write several books in a series and want to give away their first book for free while charging a premium for the next books in the series. There are still others who want the novelty of being an Amazon bestseller, and so choose categories with low competition just to obtain the badge that says their book is an Amazon bestseller. Clearly, pricing can change based on these goals. I don't suggest pricing the book too low because, as I've already mentioned, a low price may not always increase book sales. And it could drop the perceived value of your book and ultimately hurt sales. In the below paragraphs, I have set out what I believe to be the best possible prices for an ebook and paperback. But remember, the prices will vary depending on your goals.

Ebook Pricing

Amazon has been trying to standardize the pricing of ebooks on its Kindle platform. Amazon pays a royalty of 70 percent if the price of an ebook is between $2.99 and $9.99, and the royalty drops to 35 percent if the ebook is not priced within this range. So, it makes sense to price your ebook between $2.99 and $9.99 if you're looking for a higher royalty from Amazon.

As I mentioned, pricing also depends on the goals of the author. Are you trying to build your personal brand by pricing your book so its perceived value is higher? Many nonfiction authors make money not from the sales of their book but from coaching, online courses, consulting, and many other avenues. If you want the maximum number of people to read your book, then you may want to price your book based on your goals.

According to data collected by Smashwords, the best price to maximize sales is between $2.99 and $3.99.[31] The next best option is $0.99. Books priced at $3.99 on average sell 4.3 times more than those priced above $10. Books priced at $2.99 sell 4.1 times more than those priced above $10. And books priced at $0.99 sell 3.9 times more than books priced above $10. For example, my ebook is priced at $6.99, which has a probability of selling around 1.9 times more than books priced above $10.

If you want to maximize sales, the best price is $3.99, according to the Smashwords survey.

According to Tucker Max, if you want to increase perceived value, then $7.99 and $9.99 is the price range to look at.[32] The middle ground is $4.99 to $6.99. Max also suggests the best price to maximize sales is between $0.99 to $3.99. However, based on my experience and research, I believe the best price is $3.99, and the next best is $2.99. The sweet spot for many authors is $3.99.

Tucker Max's article leaves out a few important aspects of the book which affect pricing—the book-length, genre, and the credibility of the author. Obviously, books by well-known authors can be priced higher.

---

31   Mark Coker, "New Smashwords Survey Helps Authors Sell More EBooks," New Smashwords Survey Helps Authors Sell More eBooks, January 1, 1970, https://blog.smashwords.com/2013/05/new-smashwords-survey-helps-authors.html.

32   Tucker Max, "The Ultimate Guide to Book Pricing (and How to Maximize Sales)," Scribe Media, September 22, 2020, https://scribewriting.com/book-pricing-guide/.

Book pricing can be one of the most confusing aspects of self-publishing. You don't want to price your book too low or too high. If you price it too low, then you lose out on possible profit. If you price it too high, you might be pricing yourself out of the market. You want to price your book at that optimum level where the sales are maximized, and the profit is highest.

Amazon KDP has a service called 'Pricing Support.' When you upload your book onto Amazon's KDP, under 'Royalty and Pricing', you'll see an option called 'View Service'. When you click on 'View Pricing', Amazon will show you a graph of the best optimum prices based on books similar to yours. The graph shows how pricing affects your book's sales. The tool gives you the best optimum price for your book based on the book's genre and length. Some authors claim this pricing by Amazon is reliable, but I'm not sure I want to rely on it; I prefer to set my own.

Paperback Pricing

Paperbacks can also be priced according to the genre, length, and credibility of the author, just as for ebooks. The length of the paperback matters more than with ebooks because printing costs are involved. Also, longer books cost more to manufacture, so they justify a slightly higher price.

Tucker Max mentions in his article that print books are priced around $7 to $10 more than ebooks.[33] I've seen paperbacks priced at $16 more than an ebook, which is an extreme case. If you're using IngramSpark and want to discount your books for distributors to the lowest possible discounted price and accept returns, then pricing your print books higher might work.

---

33   Ibid.

A good strategy might be to price books according to other similar books in your genre, using the method I've explained above. That gives you a price that readers are already used to paying. If you have time, you could experiment with pricing. Otherwise, I suggest it's wiser to stick to a price range readers of your genre are already paying for similar books and unlikely to object to.

Audiobooks

Audiobooks can add an additional revenue stream for authors. If priced correctly, they can add significantly to the bottom line for the author.

Let's see how they're priced.

Audible is the Big Daddy retailer of audiobooks. ACX, a part of Audible, distributes to Audible, iTunes, and Amazon.

I'm now going to tell you something to make your life easier: Audible does not allow authors to price their audiobooks. Audible chooses the price for you. All you need to do is upload your files on ACX, and audible sets the price for your audiobook automatically.

ACX's website says, "Each retailer of your audiobook independently prices your product and determines such price at their sole discretion. While not always the case, the regular price on Audible for the product is generally priced based on its length, as follows:

- under 1 hour: under $7
- 1 - 3 hours: $7 - $10
- 3 - 5 hours: $10 - $20
- 5 - 10 hours: $15 - $25
- 10 - 20 hours: $20 - $30
- Over 20 hours: $25 - $35

To be clear, although the above represents general guidelines as retailers of audiobooks sold on the Audible website, Audible retains the sole discretion to set the price of the audiobooks it sells."[34]

However, if you decide to publish through an aggregator like Findaway Voices, you'll need to set your own prices. There are two prices you'll need to set: one is the retail price, and the other is the library price. The library price is generally two to three times more than the retail price because the library will distribute the book to its members.

How to Write Nonfiction by Joseph Robinson is 168 pages and is priced at $2.99 for the ebook, $19.87 for the paperback, and $14.95 for the audiobook of three hours and twelve minutes.

Dear Writer, You Need to Quit! by Becca Syme is 114 pages and is priced at $2.99 for an ebook, $9.99 for a paperback, and $14.95 for the audiobook of three hours and twenty-two minutes.

How to Write a Book by William Murphy is priced at $14.95 for the audiobook of three hours and twenty-six minutes.

As you can see from the above examples, most audiobooks in my genre that are about three hours in length are priced at $14.99. If you analyze the pricing of audiobooks in your genre, you should be able to come up with a fair price that listeners are used to paying and will happily accept.

34   "How Much Will My Audiobook Sell for in Stores?," Help.acx.com, accessed August 29, 2021, https://help.acx.com/s/article/how-much-will-my-audiobook-sell-for-in-stores.

The world of book pricing can be complex and confusing. Some authors experiment often to find their sweet spot. But I think it's important to have some sort of methodology when it comes to pricing. I hope the strategies outlined in this chapter can help you get closer to your sweet spot and help you fulfill your goals.

Chapter 8

Metadata and Writing Book Descriptions

The metadata for a book generally includes the title and subtitle of the book, book description, ISBN, price, keywords, publisher information, and publication date. The purpose of metadata is to make it easy for readers to find your book via an online search engine. If they can't or don't find your book, how can they buy it?

So, let's look at some of the most common metadata you'll need before you get started with publishing your book.

Keywords

When you upload your book on Amazon, the platform allows you to add up to seven keywords. You can also leave them blank, but it's highly beneficial to add keywords because they help in the discovery of your book via search engines. Amazon has its own search facility on its website to aid in finding books. But besides using Amazon's search facility, books can also be found via search engines. When people type in a keyword in search of a book, if your book is tagged with any of those keywords, it will show up as a product of the search. And, as we all know, the higher the visibility of your book, the higher the chances of it being bought.

But how do you go about finding the right keywords to make your book visible and show up on search results ahead of other bestselling books?

It's a fact that more than 85 percent of search traffic comes from Google, so we'll focus on Google to ensure you get high-quality keywords.

Let's first go to Google's Keyword Planner by typing https://ads.google. com/home/tools/keyword-planner in your browser.

You'll need to enter your Google username and password to get access. If you don't already have a Google account, you can easily sign up for one.

In the box that appears, enter keywords, phrases, or words closely related to your book, then click on the 'Get Results' button. Google's keyword planner tool will then give you a list of relevant keywords, along with average search volume and competition for each one. Make a list of high volume and low competition keywords. These keywords can be saved to become a vital part of your metadata.

Whenever you upload your book onto a publishing platform, you'll have your keywords ready to use. Most publishing platforms have an option to add keywords.

Using some of these keywords in your book descriptions, perhaps even in the title of your book, can also help your book become more discoverable.

Author Name

The 'author name' can be either your full name (first and last names) or your pen name. For various reasons, some authors prefer to use a pen name instead of their real name. For instance, they might write about certain topics but don't want their books to be associated with their work profiles, or they may write in another genre under another name and don't want the two to be confused. Will you use your real name or a pen name? If you're using a pen name, have a good enough reason for doing so.

Title of Your Book

In my earlier book, *How to Write Your First Nonfiction Book*, I talk in more detail about creating a title for your book. I'm assuming here that you already have a title for your book. In case you haven't already chosen one, it's time to do it now and keep it handy before you start the publishing process.

Book Description

Your book description is an important part of the publishing process. It's a valuable tool in selling your book. The book description could be added to the back cover of your book and appear on the product page too. However, the back cover has limited space, so your description might have to be shortened for the back cover. The product pages on Amazon and other online retailers allow you to add a lot more information. What should be on the book description page? Well, a short synopsis of the book, quotes from book reviews, reasons why readers should buy your book or anything else that might help your book to sell. Remember, the purpose of a book description is to help your book sell. The book description should answer the potential buyer's question as to why they should buy your book.

About the Author

Generally, information about the author appears on the back cover of a book. Readers like to know something about who has written the book. This is especially true for nonfiction writing, where the author is positioning themselves as an authority in their chosen field. Again, this information can go on the back cover of the book, the last page of the book, or even on the product page of retailers.

Categories

Categories help bookstores place your book on the right shelves. It can be devastating for sales when the book is placed on the wrong shelf, and no one reads it because it's not relevant to them. Making sure it's in the right category ensures potential buyers find your book more easily as it's visible to the right readers.

The Book Industry Study Group has created BISAC (Book Industry Standards and Communications) codes to help categorize books. It's used by several brick-and-mortar bookstores and internal databases to categorize books so they can be found easily.

A good way to find out which category your book best fits into is to find similar books to yours and see which category they are listed under on Amazon and other places. If you think those categories are relevant to your book, you can list yours under the same categories.

Author Photographs

As they say, a picture speaks a thousand words. Readers want a face they can connect with. A photo of the author allows readers to put a face to your name. Believe it or not, authors find it hard to get a good picture. I suggest checking out the photos of best-selling authors on the internet, finding one you like, and then having a photo taken in a similar style. A headshot is the most impressive and works best because you can place it in the 'About the Author' section on the back cover of your book.

ISBN

If you want your book to be available for sale with online retailers and bookstores, then you need an ISBN, which is a unique 13-digit identification code to identify your book.

ISBN stands for International Standards Book Number.

Most bookstores and online retailers insist on an ISBN.

ISBNs can be purchased from a national agency in your country that is authorized to issue ISBNs. Agencies in some countries offer ISBNs for free.

Bowker is the agency that issues ISBNs in the USA and Australia. If you are selling books in multiple countries, you don't need multiple ISBNs. However, you'll need different ISBNs for each different format of your book. For example, the ISBNs for your paperback, hardcover, and ebook are going to be different from each other. So, you'll need to purchase an ISBN for each format of your book.

The cost of an ISBN purchased from Bowker in the US is $125 per ISBN.

Amazon issues its own version of ISBN called ASIN for their Kindle books. The ASIN issued by Amazon cannot be used to publish your ebook on other platforms like Nook, Apple iBook, and Google Play.

Certain self-publishing platforms like Amazon offer a free ISBN, but this can be used only to publish on their platform. It cannot be used anywhere else.

In India, ISBNs are issued for free by Raja Rammohun Roy agency for ISBNs (isbn.gov.in). Please be aware, the agency for ISBNs in India insists that ISBNs be used only for books published in India. So, if you want your books to be published in multiple countries, then you might want to purchase your ISBNs from a different source.[35]

If you are publishing on several different platforms, then I suggest it's best to purchase your own ISBN from Bowker. If you need help with purchasing an ISBN, please contact us through our website https://www.publishedge.com/contact/

Pricing

In the previous chapter, we spoke about book pricing. If you've decided on the price for your book, add it here so that your metadata is all in one place.

Tax and Financial Information

Amazon's KDP and several self-publishing platforms require you to fill in your financial and tax information before you can publish your book. This information includes your social security number or tax identification number, bank account information, mailing address, PayPal information (if you have an account), and other tax-related information. It's best to

---

35 "FAQ," Raja Rammohun Roy National Agency for ISBN, Department of Higher Education, MHRD, Government of India, accessed August 29, 2021, https://isbn.gov.in/v2/FAQ.aspx?langid=1.

have all this information handy before you begin to upload your book on a publishing platform.

It's so important to remember that readers rely on your book's metadata to find information about your book. Having accurate metadata and storing it in one place will make the process much easier for you when you are ready to publish your book on a self-publishing platform.

Chapter 9

Back Matter and Front Matter

Sometimes, self-published books look self-published because they're missing the front and back matter we normally expect to see in a book. If you open a book published by one of the best publishing companies in the world, you'll immediately see pages such as a title page, copyright information page, a table of contents page, etc. Some might also have a dedication page, perhaps a page with a quotation or piece of poetry which the author feels represents their book. Or even a page with an author's note about some aspect of the book. Books might also include front pages for a foreword, a preface, an introduction, sometimes a chronology, an index, and some will have a resources page. Obviously, not every book needs to have all these pages, but having some of them will make your book look more professional.

Front matter refers to the pages usually found at the beginning of a book, and back matter refers to the miscellaneous pages mostly found at the back of a book. So, the front and back matter act like bookends to the main text. Let's go through some of these different types of pages in more detail and help you decide which of these pages your book needs and might benefit from.

Front Matter: Pages Usually Found at the Beginning of a Book

Title Page

The title page is just that—it sets out in large type the title of the book followed by the author's name. In most non-fiction books, the title page is generally printed in black and white. If you are going to self-publish your book, you'll probably need a typesetter to help you take care of this. However, if you have a publisher, they should do this for you so you won't have to worry about it.

Copyright Information Page

If you're a self-publishing author, you'll need to include a page showing copyright information about your book. This consists of the copyright symbol, author name, the name of your organization or imprint, and your business address.

Table of Contents (TOC)

Most books have a TOC of some sort as it helps readers navigate through content. A simple way to insert a table of contents in a Word document is by clicking on 'References' on the Word menu bar, then selecting 'Insert Table of Contents'. This will automatically insert a TOC, *provided the title of each chapter is formatted as a heading.*

If you're using a professional typesetter, I suggest asking them to add a table of contents for you rather than trying to do it in Word yourself. It's something they can do with ease as they go about their job of typesetting your book.

Foreword

Someone other than the author, often a well-known writer or, in the case of non-fiction books, a high-profile industry expert, usually writes the foreword to a book. The purpose of a foreword is to introduce the author to the world. A foreword is a marketing tool more than anything else, as it acts as an endorsement by an authority or expert and is designed to add credibility to the author and recommend their work.

Does every book need a foreword? No, they're often unnecessary, especially with fiction books. In fact, lots of books, even bestselling ones, don't have forewords.

But if you do decide to go with a foreword, then you should approach someone whom you respect and admire and invite them to write it.

Think back to the time when you were in the research phase of writing your book, when, hopefully, you made an effort to follow my advice about connecting with important people in your industry.

This is one of those times when such connections could pay off as one of those people you connected with might make an ideal candidate to write you the perfect foreword.

But try to pick someone who's a good writer as well as an authority!

The last thing you need is an expert who can't write well. That could cause problems because if you pick an expert who isn't such a great writer, you risk hurting their ego if you ultimately choose not to publish their foreword.

I recommend doing a little research on their writing skills before approaching them. Read their blog posts or any articles or books they've written to get an idea about their capabilities.

When asking someone to write a foreword for your book, make sure you make your expectations clear, but try not to be too pushy.

There are really no rules as to how a foreword should be written, so long as it's well-written and enhances the credibility of the author. Ideally, it should aim to persuade the reader to read the rest of the book. As mentioned earlier, the foreword is mainly a marketing tool and should be treated as such in order to benefit you in promoting your book.

Use the foreword wisely if you choose to include one. However, there's no need to add one just for the heck of it.

Prologue

When I think about books with prologues, two examples spring to mind: one is Richard Branson's autobiography *Losing My Virginity*; the other is Peter Lynch's book *One Up on Wall Street*. In their prologues, both authors talk briefly about incidents that happened on specific days of their lives. This serves to set the scene for readers, as well as the tone and mood for the chapters that follow.

For instance, Lynch narrates incidents that happened on October 16, 1987, and how they shaped his thinking going forward as well as the lessons he took from them. In these cases, the prologues help set readers' expectations for the rest of the book. If you believe that a background story could benefit your readers as they read on, then a prologue could make an interesting and effective addition to your book.

Preface

An author's relationship with their readers starts from the moment the reader picks up their book. Some writers capitalize on this by including a preface at the start of their book.

But what is a preface? Well, it's been said that 'the game behind the game is more interesting than the game', and a preface gives authors a chance to add interest and deepen understanding for readers by explaining the story behind their book.

For instance, it can outline the reasons why the author chose to write the book, their motivation, and the effort put in behind the scenes to complete the book.

Acknowledgments

I remember a client of mine asking me where within her book could she acknowledge the contribution of her photographer. This was quite reasonable as authors usually take several months, sometimes years, to write a book, and get help from several people along the way, whose assistance they want to acknowledge.

While the acknowledgment may not matter so much to you, the people whose names are mentioned will feel special at being acknowledged for playing a role in the making of your book.

Introduction

Most people, whether online or offline, generally read the introduction before buying a book. That's the reason why your introduction should aim to encourage the reader to buy your book.

In my experience, many authors don't take the introduction seriously enough, filling it with fluff that fails to draw readers in.

Some writing coaches suggest that the introduction should be kept short. I'm not sure if I agree with that advice: Introductions should be just the right length to keep your audience excited and entice readers to keep turning the pages.

Back Matter: Pages Found at the Back of a Book

Now, let's look at the different types of pages that are usually found at the end of the book:

Index

Indexes have appeared as part of printed books for a long time. An index is a reference tool that gives readers an option to go back and forth within the book to reference specific information.

Not only is an index useful or even necessary in some circumstances, but it also makes the book look more professional and well-organized.

You can easily create an index for a Word document, or you can ask your editor to do it for you. Some editors might charge a small fee for providing this service, but you can learn to do it yourself—it's not as complicated as it might sound.

Appendix

An appendix is a place where any additional information that might be beneficial to your reader can be added. It can take up several pages, depending on how much information is added to it. For instance, if you mention an article you've written in the body of the book, you can reproduce the article in the appendix instead of mentioning a web link. That way, the reader can turn to the appendix of the book and read the article right away rather than accessing it via a web link.

Appendices can include almost anything—articles, letters, research reports, case studies, charts, images, and pretty much any information that doesn't fit into the body of the book. The information in the appendix should be supplemental information, perhaps concerning something you mentioned in the body of the book and want to elaborate on which, if included in the chapter, might disrupt its flow.

Although the appendix option allows you to add as much information as you want, it's important to avoid adding things that aren't relevant or supplemental to the book as a whole.

Glossary

If, in your book, you use technical terms that your audience may not immediately understand, the glossary is the place to record them and define their meaning. For example, if you write a book on finance, you might use phrases like 'working capital,' 'margin of safety,' and so on. You don't want to force your reader to guess their meaning or have to put down your book to go and look them up online. You can easily prevent that by adding any industry terms or jargon (if you can't avoid using it) to the glossary. The glossary is usually arranged in alphabetical order, or sometimes there may be a sub-glossary for each chapter or section so that the relevant words and terms are even easier to find.

Bibliography/References

A bibliography is the place where you can mention any reference sources you used in writing your book. It's where all the information, such as useful links to research reports, books, and any other sources used as reference or research information for your book, can be listed. The correct method for citing sources in the bibliography varies from style guide to style guide, so make sure to use the appropriate one, which could be MLA, Chicago, AMA, or any other style that you've used throughout the book.

Resources

This is sometimes called 'Further Reading,' and is the place where you can recommend more books you think might interest your readers. If you want to recommend a list of books, tools, software, or other material you feel might benefit readers, this is the section where they can be listed.

Also, there are times when authors mention tools, websites, or books they consider might be helpful or of interest to readers in the body of the book. It's always a good idea to collate and organize these into a list in the resources section.

Having reviewed all the different types of pages that can be included in books, you must decide which ones are necessary for your book and which can be left out. Few books contain all the pages discussed here. Whether certain pages are included or not is based on the author's preference. If you're self-publishing, you have the freedom to go against the grain and add sections that are not mentioned here if you think they make your book more interesting.

The purpose of this chapter is to give you, the new author, an idea of the different types of pages authors can choose to use in a book and their purpose for doing so. Some have little more than novelty value, while others can help promote your book, benefit the reader, and provide a great overall reading experience.

Chapter 10

Importance of an Index

Rarely do authors talk about the index in their books; it's a useful navigation tool and makes a book look well-organized. But it's hardly the main event. I've seen many self-published paperbacks with no index, but I believe paperbacks should have an index and benefit from having one. It helps readers easily find any information from the text they want to refer back to. Most ebook readers generally have a search option, so an index isn't really necessary in an ebook. I usually don't add an index in my ebooks because of the available search option, but I've found it's useful for readers if I add an index to my paperbacks.

Sometimes, an index also acts as a sales tool, as readers go through the index to find interesting concepts in your book.

Below are the purposes of an index.

Find Information

One of the primary purposes of an index is to find information. In a paperback, there's no search option as there is in an ebook. So, if readers want to find specific information, their only option is to go through the index in the paperback.

Reviewers also might want to go back and check out relevant information when they are writing a book review.

Another purpose of an index is for potential readers to get a quick preview of the content of your book. Sometimes, we just want a quick preview of what's in the book. In that context, an index can be a wonderful addition to your paperback. Readers expect an index, and without one, I think a paperback looks incomplete and less professional.

Professional indexers consider creating an index to be an art form. There is an art to creating a good index. However, creating one is not as complicated as you might think. Anyone can learn to create an index, and I've outlined a step-by-step process below to show you how to do it.

What Does an Index Include?

An index is an accessibility guide. It's designed to help the reader locate information easily and quickly. It's always structured in alphabetical order, and it's an ordered arrangement of the most substantive terms in a book.

To craft an exceptional index for your paperback, first, pick two or three bestselling paperbacks. Study the index in each book. Note the structure and the ease with which you found the terms you were looking for.

The following are the key components of an index:

- Terms
- Headings
- Subheadings
- Sub-subheadings
- Indents

- Locators
- Cross-references
- Entry blocks

Now, let's look at what each of these contains.

Terms

The most fundamental parts of an index are terms. These are words, phrases, or symbols that represent a concept. The terms are the information readers are trying to locate. Apart from the locators, everything else we see on a page showing an index are terms.

Headings

A heading is a single top-level topic appearing in the index. They're also described as main entries or main headings.

Subheadings

A subheading is a single entry under a main heading. It's also known as a subdivision or subentry. A subheading is usually indented; it's justified to the right directly beneath the main heading.

Sub-Subheadings

A sub-subheading is a heading at the third level. Indexing software provides six levels. But, in practice, indexers hardly ever go beyond this third level. It's also indented and is justified to the right below the subheading.

Indents

As mentioned earlier, indents show the position/level of sub and sub-subheadings. They're also used for turnover (that's when some words are too long to fit the column width). It's vital to use two different sizes for these two different indent types so readers can differentiate them with ease.

Locators

A locator shows the reader where to find the information they seek. Page numbers, figure numbers, and URLs are locators. When the content being sought extends over more than a page, you'll need to use a locator range.

As an example, let's say the topic of goalsetting is mentioned several times in your book on pages 67-70. In your index, 67-70 will be the locator range—the pages where the references to goalsetting appear. It's a range because it's more than a single-page reference. A locator string is formed when you attach several locators to the heading. For example: Goalsetting 67, 68, 69. The page numbers are called locator strings.

Cross-References

A cross-reference directs the user to another heading in the index. There you'll see the terms used in indexing to denote a cross-reference or a series of them—that's where the same topic or other topics related to it are mentioned in several places throughout the book.

The most common terms used indexing are:

'See . . .': For example, let's say you look up the word 'comma' in the index. But 'comma' is not listed as the main heading but as a sub-subheading under the main heading 'Punctuation,' and then under its subheading 'Commonly used punctuation marks.' So, the 'see' that follows 'comma' is telling you to go to the main heading 'Punctuation,' then its subheading below 'Commonly used punctuation marks' to find references to 'comma'. There, you'll find the relevant locators to enable you to find all the references to 'comma' within the book.

'See also . . .': This refers you to other terms that appear in the book which are related to the one you're searching for in the index. For example, say you look up the word 'birds.' Then, you might see 'birds see also reptiles.' This tells you that birds and reptiles are subjects that are related to each other *and within the context of the book*. Or you might look up 'birds' and find the entry 'birds see also parrots, eagles, and so on listed with the relevant locators. This is because 'birds' is what indexers call a 'parent term' for all different kinds of birds.

Other common cross-reference terms you might see in an index are 'See under...', 'See also under . . .' , which guide you to another part of the index relevant to your search. You might also see 'q.v.' This Latin abbreviation stands for *quod vide* (which see) and applies to a specific word or expression within a heading or subheading, indicating that it can be turned to as a separate heading in the same index.

Entry Blocks

An entry block is a 'unit' of an index. It refers to all the text under a single heading. In other words, a unit refers to the subheadings, sub-subheadings, locators, and references that make up an entry.

We've explored the key parts of an index. Now, let's look at what to include and what to exclude from an index.

Before you can craft a helpful index, you need to think like a reader. An index must guide your reader to the most vital parts of your book quickly and easily, so you need to make sure your index is user-friendly.

So, you could start with your TOC and then check each page where you've written about a particular theme or concept. You must comb through each page, identifying the most vital concepts and noting them down. Remember, the indexing covers only the body of the text.

What to Exclude from Your Index?

The following is a handy list of the specifics not to include:

Glossary
Bibliography
Table of Contents
Epigraphs
Acknowledgments
Appendix
Notes
Source citations
Non-essential terms

You use indexes, right? Think of the best ones and model yours on them. The best ones have a general heading, and underneath are key concepts. The key concepts act like keys that readers can use to access more content. So, what to include in an index is a process of prioritization and elimination.

Say you've written a book titled *Mastering Martial Arts*. In it, you've profiled ten different arts, and one of them is Brazilian Jiu-Jitsu. In this context, one area your index must cover is 'Locks.' So, you'll have a block entry covering locks. Cross-reference it to relevant parts of the book where you've mentioned locks. You need to do this even if they're mentioned under a different art within the text, say, as used in Judo, and even what they're called in Japanese!

You should include entries that reflect the way you would access the book if you were a reader (and not the writer).

Indexing should be the last thing to do in the book. You can't get started on the index while you're still making adjustments to the text.

Study each chapter carefully, as you'll need to decide which are the most vital terms—the terms that a potential user is most likely to look for when trying to learn about specific concepts.

In the preceding paragraph, we looked at what to include and what to exclude from an index. Now, let's proceed to what's involved in creating an index for your paperback.

How to Create an Index for Your Paperback?

You're curious about how long the index should be, right? Unfortunately, there's no one size fits all tip. The index should be as long as necessary to serve the reader, but no longer. The rule of thumb is that it shouldn't be over 5 percent of the number of pages in the book.

You don't need to capitalize index entries unless they refer to proper nouns. References to images should be in bold or italics.

I suggest you take advantage of MS Word's index function. It's simple to use once you get started. But a word of warning: don't use the Word index option unless you're also going to publish your book in that format.

If you're using another publishing format, MS Word's pagination may not transfer successfully.

You'll start by painstakingly going through the text and noting down all the important terms. As you're doing this, focus on the words the reader is likely to use when searching for information about the topic.

You'll also need to distinguish between the key terms (main entries) and the subordinate terms (subentries). Then, use the following simple steps in Word:

Mark Basic Entries
Mark Special Entries
Insert Index
Review and Change

While going through the text again, go to 'References'. Under 'Index', click on 'Ark Entry'. You'll see a dialog box. If you need to, you can edit the text shown to the exact word you want, which reflects how the reader would search. To capture a repeated main entry term, select 'Mark All'. To mark a single occurrence of a term, select 'Mark'.

After the selection, you'll see a bracketed XE notation in the text. To make it invisible, click on the Paragraph tab in the Home tab.

Choose the appropriate entry from the 'Mark Entry' dialog box to create different entries. You can use that to create subentries, but there shouldn't be more than one subentry to a subentry. That's the main entry and two subentries. And to create a cross-reference, simply choose it from the dialog box. To create a figure, table, or image reference, highlight it and click 'Mark Entry'. Fill in the right entry and select italic or bold.

Repeat the process as needed, and when you're satisfied, go through the index to be sure it's exactly what you had in mind. Then, click the section of the book where you'd like to have it. Then, click 'Insert Index' in the 'References' tab of the Index section. Then, select the style, the number of columns, and page number alignment. Click OK, and you're done!

In the preceding paragraphs, we explored what's an index, what to include, and what not to include in your paperback index, and we also looked at tips for crafting an awesome index.

Finally, we wrapped things up by looking at how to use MS Word to craft your index. As you can see, crafting a good index is a vital part of creating an outstanding paperback, and it's not at all a difficult process in Word.

Chapter 11

Copyrights

Copyrights are an area of confusion for many self-published authors. Whether you register the copyrights of your book with a government agency or not, it is protected by copyright law. The moment you write the book, you automatically become the copyright owner of your book.

Copyright law exists to prohibit anyone from copying and distributing your work, or part of it, without your permission, even if you don't register your content with the government's copyright office. In fact, in most countries, your content is automatically copyrighted the moment you create it. So, if someone copies your work without giving you proper credit, you can sue them. However, the onus is on you to prove the work belongs to you.

So, copyright prohibits people from copying and distributing the work of the author without permission from the copyright holder.

As I mentioned earlier, copyright laws can vary depending on the country. In the US, authors own the copyright to their work the moment they create it until seventy years after their death.

In India, too, copyright is automatic and is valid until sixty years after the death of the author. According to the *Handbook of Copyright Law* issued by the Indian government, "Acquisition of copyright is automatic, and it does not require any formality. However, a Certificate of Registration of Copyright and the entries made therein serve as *prima facie* evidence in a court of law with reference to dispute relating to ownership of copyright."[36]

The UK also has automatic copyright protection, with works protected for seventy years after the death of the author.

The UK Government website says, "You get copyright protection automatically—you don't have to apply or pay a fee. There isn't a register of copyright works in the UK."[37] The website further goes on to say, "You can mark your work with the copyright symbol ©, your name, and the year of creation. Whether you mark the work or not doesn't affect the level of protection you have."[38]

Copyright is protected in other countries besides your home country through various international agreements, so check what applies to you according to the country you're in.

---

36 "Copyright Law in India," Copyright Law in India - Copyright Office, Copyright act, accessed August 30, 2021, https://www.legalserviceindia. com/article/l195-Copyright-Law-in-India.html.
37 Government Digital Service, "How Copyright Protects Your Work," GOV.UK (GOV.UK, November 18, 2015), https://www.gov.uk/copyright.
38 Ibid.

In the US, you can register the copyrights to your book through the US Copyrights Office.[39] There are also various services providers like CopyrightsNOW who help you register your copyrights for a fee.[40]

---

39 U.S. Copyright Office, "Welcome to the U.S. Copyright Office," U.S. Copyright Office | U.S. Copyright Office, accessed August 30, 2021, https://www.copyright.gov/.

40 "Copyrightsnow.com," CopyrightsNow, accessed August 30, 2021, http://www.copyrightsnow.com/.

Chapter 12

How to Sell Your Books?

Selling books is one of the most challenging tasks for self-published authors. Publishing a book and making it available for sale is the easy part. It's very difficult to put a fixed number on it as some authors are clearly bestsellers and sell lots of books. But there is research to suggest the average number of sales for most self-published authors is less than 250 copies in their entire lifetime, leave alone a year![41]

But don't let that put you off. The biggest reason most self-published authors don't sell many books is because they don't promote their books. They have a poor marketing strategy or, even worse, no marketing strategy at all. If you want to sell more books, you've got to have a strong focus on sales and marketing. It sounds daunting, but it's not as difficult as it sounds—there are lots of online tools out there to help you do it with ease, often for free. In this chapter, I've listed a basic step-by-step process to help you build a solid marketing strategy.

---

41 Chris A. Baird, "How Many Books Does the Average Self Published Author Sell?" Self-Publishing Made Easy Now!, September 9, 2020, https://selfpublishingmadeeasynow.com/how-many-books-does-the-average-self-published-author-sell/.

Step 1: Build a Mailing List

There's a well-known saying in online business: 'The Money is in the List.' It's used to describe the important relationship between an email list of subscribers and long-term success at marketing your product online—in this case, books. The size of your list will determine how much money you make from your online sales. The best marketers in the world are constantly building their mailing list, which in turn allows them to build a relationship with their audience before even selling them anything.

When I talk about a mailing list, I mean an 'opt-in' mailing list. You want to entice your audience to *willingly* subscribe to your mailing list. Seth Godin calls it 'permission-based marketing.' In internet marketing lingo, it's called an opt-in mailing list. What is an opt-in mailing list? An opt-in list is when someone visits your website and enters their email address subscribing to your newsletter. You've received specific permission to mail them information. It's that simple.

Today, most of us get more emails than we can read. We might almost think that most people don't want to receive emails at all! It's true that many people don't want to give their email addresses, but if you're sharing information that is beneficial, informative, and entertaining, people will look forward to your emails. It satisfies people's psychological needs—and we all have it—to know what's in it for them. Another reason people want to receive information is because they want to get to know you better before they make a buying decision. Authors have the opportunity to do things like share a sneak peek of their book, tell subscribers the motivation behind writing the book, and about the behind-the-scenes making of the book. Don't be afraid to reveal your personality because your personality cannot be copied, and readers are generally attracted to an author's personality and their style of writing. If you are an open person, you can also share information about your life. All these things help create a lasting bond between you and your reader.

Collecting Contact Information

There's a lot of software out there to help you add an opt-in form to your website and automate the tedious process of collecting contact information. You can also set up autoresponders, so as soon as someone subscribes to your mailing list, they receive an automatic welcome response from you. You don't need to know anything about coding or programming to do it. Do you know you can even add an opt-in form to your Facebook page?

Mailchimp and Aweber are the most popular software packages available for setting up your mailing list.

Although I use Mailchimp, I believe Aweber is worth considering, too, as it has some very beautiful templates to choose from.

Here's a list of some popular software packages:

1. MAILCHIMP

For the beginner, Mailchimp offers a free version.

PROS
- It's considered one of the easiest tools to master. Importing and exporting lists is easy.
- Offers a 100 percent free account with limited access to features.
- Good for sporadic, limited newsletters to be sent to few contacts.
- Payments can be made as you go or on a monthly subscription.

➢ Offers numerous integrations. Enables you to connect to Instapage, Facebook, WordPress, Hubspot, LeadPages, and most other marketing tools.

CONS

➢ Their form builder is very basic.
➢ Most of their features are extremely basic.

2. AWEBER

A very popular email marketing tool used by most bloggers and internet marketers.

PROS

➢ Ease of creation. Aweber has a very user-friendly navigation system. It's a flexible marketing tool and is fast. It has an easily automated email campaign creator with a drag-and-drop editor.
➢ Aweber has more than 150 customizable templates.
➢ Analytics. Aweber offers easy-to-read charts for an analysis of your email campaign. You can get data on which links were clicked, how much revenue was generated, etc. This helps in targeting future campaigns. Subscriber management, tracking, and segmentation are neat too.
➢ Delivery of mails. Aweber has the maximum reach in terms of delivery of emails. This software boasts a 98 percent success rate in terms of reaching people's inboxes because of very reliable Aweber servers.

CONS

➢ Aweber does not provide an option for an embedded video in the email. That's not a major issue, but if a video has to be hosted, you'd need to be on the blog or video-sharing website and then link it via the email.

3. GETRESPONSE

With a clear landing page, GetResponse is more than just an email autoresponder.

PROS
> - The comprehensive reporting is very analytical, with easy-to-read graphs that enable further optimization of campaigns.
> - The contacts section of GetResponse allows you to easily add custom fields, copy contacts, conduct searches, and has flexible templates.
> - GetResponse can track the number of subscribers who open emails, unsubscribe, click on links, how many people visit your website via the link in the email and give reasons why people unsubscribe.

CONS
> - They have live chat support but don't offer twenty-four-hour phone support.
> - The multimedia library is not particularly user-friendly.
> - The user interface could also do with some improvement.

They offer a thirty-day free trial that includes 250 contacts and unlimited emails.

4. ACTIVECAMPAIGN

Considered a gem in the automation world of marketing, this is quite a well-designed software.

PROS

➢ ActiveCampaign helps you create a seamless and engaging email on an easy-to-use platform. Known for its great user interface.

➢ It combines email newsletters, marketing automation, and CRM (Customer Relationship Management) into an automation tool.

➢ Easy onboarding of customers and sending of coupons using autoresponders.

CONS

➢ Needs more upgrading in the CRM and email builder. For example, searching for a lead in CRM requires you to scroll down endlessly.

➢ It does not have native integration with third-party tools.

Out of all the above, I prefer to use Aweber or Mailchimp. Some authors have begun to use SendFox as well because it's much cheaper than the other options listed here. If you're on a tight budget, why not give it a try?

How to Find Subscribers?

The two primary sources to encourage subscribers to sign up to your mailing list are:

1. Social Media
2. Search Engines

The social media site I use to very effectively generate leads is:

Facebook

Paid ads. There are a few ways paid ads can be used to build a mailing list. One is to get viewers to click on the link and land on your website or landing page where they can enter their email. The other option is to create a lead-generation ad where subscribers can fill up a form without leaving Facebook. I tend to get more leads with Facebook's lead generation ad because Facebook automatically fills in information based on the viewer's Facebook profile, so it's a convenient process for the subscriber. Also, Facebook's algorithm identifies users with a habit of subscribing to newsletters. However, I've noticed the open rate of emails is much lower with lead generation ads compared to when people visit your website and enter their contact information there.

The cost of placing ads on Facebook is a bit cheaper compared to using Google AdWords.

Search Engines

Before social media, search engines were one of the predominant ways for people to find information. They are still very relevant today in marketing.

There are two ways in which you can use search engines to promote your business: Search Engine Optimization (SEO) and Search Engine Marketing (SEM).

> - **SEO:** As the term states, optimization of your site is key here and can help your site get higher rankings on search engines. Keywords, meta tags, and internal and external links can help you achieve this goal.
> - **SEM:** This involves buying ads related to certain specific keywords using a bidding system.

In other words, you can get website visitors either organically or by placing ads on search engines.

Step 2: Build a Relationship with Your Subscribers

The single biggest trick I've learned in online marketing is automation. It can save you time, money and can help you make friends as if on autopilot.

Almost all email software has something called an autoresponder. It allows you to pre-load a sequence of emails to be sent automatically to your email subscribers when they sign up to your list.

For example, if John subscribes to my newsletter, he automatically gets a welcome email, another email after three days, and so on. This means I'm building a relationship with my audience on autopilot, without investing a single minute of my time other than writing the initial sequence of emails.

When you think of the alternative—maybe writing the same email every time to 100 different people, you can see it makes sense to automate. One-on-one selling and one-on-one relationship building only takes you so far. The secret to exponential growth is automation. And it all starts with your mailing list. Many people are so driven by social media, they forget the basics of direct marketing—money is in the list! Getting people on your list might seem like a challenge, but the harder part comes after they're on it. This is when the relationship between author and reader really begins. Think of it as a romance. In college, for instance, when you get someone's phone number, you know the job isn't done—you have to woo them. You still need to call them, get to know them, and provide them with the happiness they crave before you can even think of asking them to marry you. So, the art of selling is very similar to that of romance!

The purpose of sending autoresponders is to build relationships. If you watch television, you'll know that the biggest, most popular shows are reality shows. We live in an era of reality television. If you check social media, the profiles getting the highest attention are of people who share personal information. That shows how much people out there *want* to hear your story and how your experiences can benefit them. So, why not tell them your story? Use emotion and life experiences, but don't overdo it—maintain a balance, and keep your personal security in mind at all times.

Step 3: Ask for the Sale

Once you build a sizable mailing list and have made the effort to build a relationship with your subscribers, it's time to ask for the sale. Sometimes, we're so conditioned not to sell, we don't even ask for the sale. But if you don't ask for the sale, it's highly unlikely anyone will even buy your book. Asking for the sale can simply be a polite nudge, asking your subscribers to purchase your book if they haven't already done so. If you've priced your book right and you've created a good product, ask for the sale politely and confidently by sending them an email with a link to one of the online stores where they can buy your book.

Marketing is one of the cornerstones of selling books and positioning yourself as a bestselling author. Without good marketing, you're unlikely to sell many books. I have another book exclusively focused on how to sell books. You may want to purchase that book and take your marketing seriously—if you want to sell books by the truckload. As authors, we spend a lot of time writing and publishing a book. If we spent a fraction of that time in marketing, we might sell many more books. So, to sum up, along with writing, producing, and publishing, marketing is also an important part of being a self-published author. Authors who promote themselves sell far more books than authors who publish and hope things will just happen. I hope you're one of those authors who makes sales happen!

Chapter 13

Author Platform

Author branding is an important part of selling books. Sometimes, readers buy books based on the reputation of the author. This is especially true for nonfiction books. An *author platform* is a popular concept in author branding.

An author platform is the author's online territory. It acts as the central hub that is easily accessible to readers, a place where the author can showcase and promote all the different expressions of their work. It helps the author position themselves as an authority in their chosen field. Most importantly, it gives the author the ability to influence an audience to buy from them. Eventually, the author's platform should create a community of followers who respect, admire, and support the author's work.

Why Is Having a Platform So Important?

- It provides an area where the author can build their personal brand.
- It helps build trust with an audience before asking for a sale.
- It generates a community of loyal followers who will support and buy from the author.

- It increases proximity to the author's audience and provides opportunities to obtain feedback and carry out highly specific research.

If you're an author, then a platform is the place where you can show off your writing, promote and sell your books, and any related services, such as consultancy, training, coaching, or public speaking. It's up to you how you choose to make your platform work for you. My advice is to get creative in promoting yourself as an expert in your field—with a view of growing the number of your followers and, ultimately, your book sales.

An author platform can include:

- Opt-in mailing list
- A website or blog
- Guest columns on online and offline publications
- Book reviews
- Featured articles and interviews
- Media mentions
- Speaking engagements
- Videos
- Podcasts
- Social media

What Is an Opt-in Mailing List?

As we discussed in the previous chapter, an opt-in mailing list is a compilation of the contact information of all the people who have granted you explicit permission to email them through their subscription to your website.

One of the most popular ways to collect this type of subscriber information is to place a form on your website and invite visitors to subscribe to your newsletter. You can increase the chances of them doing this by enticing them with a 'bribe' known in the business as a 'lead magnet,' which might be an e-book, a checklist, white paper, or almost anything that your reader perceives as valuable.

Opt-in Mailing List versus Social Media

One of the most common questions I get asked is: "Should I build a website, mailing list, or a social media platform?"

Well, while a website and a mailing list are assets you own and control, social media is not entirely under your control.

Here are my four main reasons why a mailing list scores over social media:

1. Your opt-in email list is yours. *You own it.*
2. It's more personal and intimate than social media.
3. You make the rules.
4. Social media is not under your control. Facebook and other social networks can change the rules at any time.

Do I need a website?

Another question I regularly get asked is: "Do authors need a website to promote their books?"

A website is a brand asset—it's something that's uniquely yours—you own it. I would describe a website as a hub, the central point from which you promote your book and build a community that will continue to grow along with your writing career.

Although you may choose to create a community through a closed group on Facebook, having a website as your central hub still helps, so visitors can read your articles, subscribe to your mailing list, and, most importantly, buy your books.

Guest Columns on Online and Offline Publications

One of the best ways to leverage your platform is by writing guest columns on online and offline publications. Many blogs and magazines are looking for content, and as an author, this offers you an opportunity to demonstrate your value to new audiences. Sometimes, an opportunity to write a guest column is as simple as shooting out an email and asking if you can write an article for that publication. For people to buy from you, they must know you. What better way than a guest column?

Interviews

Publishing a book can attract media interest and interview possibilities in print publications, blogs, magazines, radio, and even on TV. Blogs, magazines, and media publications like to interview experts on any relevant subject matter. By writing a book, you've positioned yourself as an expert on your topic. Pitching to media publications can help you get interviewed and gain you and your book some free publicity.

Book Reviews

Book reviews inspire confidence in prospective readers. We live in a culture where people rely on reviews before they buy a book. Several websites publish book reviews—some charge a fee, while others are free. You may have to contact the individual publication and submit a copy of your book for them to write a review.

Videos

We know from our own experience that, while we might skip reading something on a website, we're more likely to click on a video. A short video is a great publicity and marketing tool. It's such a familiar format yet so endlessly versatile. Remember those guest columns, featured articles, and interviews we were talking about earlier? This is the place to make them come alive—to draw readers and new visitors into your universe!

Podcasts

Hundreds of people are creating podcasts every day. Many regular podcasts draw in thousands of listeners every episode and have huge fan bases across the world. Some of these podcasters invite guests to their show. By being on their show, you become visible to their audience and have an opportunity to attract some new followers. Another option is to have your own podcast and build a fan base around your podcast.

An author platform can be one of the best investments in creating an author's personal brand. It can be daunting for authors to line up their ducks in a row all at once. But once you start building one block at a time, the process gets easier as you go. You'll soon get used to making a little progress in growing your brand every day.

Chapter 14

How to Sell Books Using Amazon Advertising?

Mastering Amazon advertising is an indispensable skill if you're self-publishing.

In this chapter, I'll share the salient points you need to know about using Amazon ads to sell more books. It's a simple process, and you don't need prior experience. You can set up your ad campaign in minutes.

We will explore three major themes:

1. The benefits and who qualifies
2. The advertising solutions available
3. Running an Amazon ad campaign

So, what are the benefits of Amazon advertising, and who qualifies to use them?

What makes Amazon ads amazing is the fact they're targeted. They help direct your ads to people who are most likely to buy your book.

The following are the benefits of Amazon advertising:

- Get started driving sales of new releases as soon as they're published
- Attract new users through 'backlist campaigns' (see below)
- Leverage genres, titles, and authors to target new users
- Easily track sales and performance metrics

A backlist campaign is one conducted for a book that's been on the market for at least one year.

So, who qualifies? If you have a retail relationship or are using Kindle Direct Publishing, then you qualify. It's a service that's available for book vendors in North America, Europe, the Middle East, and the Asia Pacific. You can access the services at https://advertising.amazon.com/books

Now, let's explore the advertising solutions available.

Amazon Advertising Solutions for Book Vendors

There are two solutions available:

- Sponsored Products
- Lockscreen Ads (available only in the US)

Sponsored Products is Cost per Click (CPC) advertising, a form of advertising that allows you to promote your books by listing each one on Amazon. People searching for related keywords or viewing similar products are likely to see your ad.

CPC is a system where you only pay when a prospect or buyer clicks on your ads. It's sometimes called Pay Per Click and is one of the cornerstones of Amazon ads. So, you're not being charged per impression; you're only charged when people show interest by clicking. Plus, you control your budget. That's to say, you can plan what you want to spend on each ad for your book.

This begs the question, what is the Cost Per Click?

The system is budget-friendly, and it enables you to control your ad spend. And that's very important. Let's say you set a bid for $0.05. That's the amount Amazon would charge you each time someone clicks on your ad. If 1000 people clicked the ad, you'll still only pay $50.

Sponsored ads can appear on different parts of a page. They can be shown at the top, close to the search bar, at the bottom, or in the middle of the screen. How they are positioned is a function of the bid, keywords, and relevancy.

The sponsored ad creative is automatically generated for you. You can even use the option of selling in other countries, even those whose language you don't speak. The system will automatically craft the ad creatives for you, thus increasing the reach of your ads.

Lockscreen Ads are more targeted than sponsored ads. They're shown to prospects when they're using their Kindle e-readers or Fire Tablets. That's when they 'unlock' their screen—hence the name of the product. The ads are shown by genre to readers at times when they're most likely to download them. They're displayed on the home screens and the device lock screens.

You're now familiar with Sponsored Products and Lockscreen Ads. So, let's proceed to the mechanics of setting up an ad.

How to Run and Manage an Amazon Ad Campaign

https://advertising.amazon.com/books

Type in the URL above, and you'll be prompted to enter the country you're located in. Once you've selected that, you'll be presented with options such as:

I have a Seller Central Account
I have a brand account
I represent a brand . . .

Once your account is set up, choose the option to use sponsored ads. This will walk you through four simple phases: settings, ad format, products, and bidding. It's a user-friendly process, but if you need any help while you're going through any of the phases, click on the 'i' button beside each stage of the process.

There are four simple things to do.

1. Decide the duration of your campaign. You can even opt for an open-ended campaign. Decide your budget.
2. Determine the keywords you're going to use.
3. Select the book you want to advertise and set the bid.
4. Launch your campaign.

There are tools you can use to help keep track of how well your campaign is performing. It's super-easy to tweak any of the variables at any time. You're free to set your price, but it's smart to find out what the average CPC is for the keywords you intend to use. The reason is that the more competitive your bids, the more likely they'll yield the intended results. You can also set automatic bids, an option I generally go for because I want the maximum number of clicks.

The beautiful thing is that you get to decide how much you want to spend. So, you can adjust it based on performance and your strategy. If you're using the ad to build a list by selling an affordable book, so long as you break even, it's a good deal. Fortunately, the system is so simple and automated, you can tweak the variables as often as you like.

Before I conclude, let's look at the bidding process. You'll obviously want to be careful about how much you're spending! And I'm sure you'd like to know how easy it is to manage a campaign. When it comes to bidding, you have three options: Fixed bids, Dynamic bids—up and won, and Dynamic bids—down only.

Fixed bids allow you to pre-select the amount you'd like to spend. Dynamic bids are when the Amazon ad system helps you decide what the bids should be, based on how likely your book will sell.

Dynamic bids—down only: The system automatically lowers your bid when the probability that you'll sell is low.

Dynamic bids—up and down: The system automatically raises your bid when the likelihood that you'll sell is higher.

It's smart to select Dynamic bids—up and down, as it can help increase your conversion rate and make more sales. The conversion rate of those who responded positively to your campaign is expressed as a percentage of the total number of people exposed to your ad. For instance, if 1,000 people saw your ad and 100 clicked it and bought your book, your conversation rate is 10 percent.

You can turn an ad on or off as you like.

The dashboard provides a status for each ad such as:

Incomplete
Delivering
Scheduled
Paused
Payment failure
Out of budget
Suspended
Ended
Archived

Amazon ads can be enhanced by leveraging analytics. Sometimes, results take time, and you might need to be patient before seeing substantial results. But once they start to come in, you can use them as part of your advertising and marketing strategy going forward.

Closing Thoughts

Now that we've come to the end of this book, let's spend some time looking back at everything we've covered in these chapters. Looking back, we've covered a lot of ground, and you should have all the information and guidance you'll need to self-publish your book.

I hope I've given you the information needed to go ahead and take the plunge into self-publishing. As I've already mentioned in earlier chapters, if you follow my step-by-step instructions and detailed guidance and do your very best to publish a book that looks as if it's been professionally produced, you'll be well on your way to successfully establishing yourself as a self-published author.

For myself, the author of this self-published book and several other successful ones, I can personally testify to the great feeling of satisfaction and pride—not to mention the thrill—that comes with that. That is why I have written this book—so that I can share my experience and knowledge directly with you, the reader, author, and would-be self-publisher. My purpose throughout the book has been to take the anxiety out of what at first might seem a daunting, complicated process by breaking it down into a series of simple, clearly explained steps you can follow until you're ready to hit PUBLISH.

In this book, I've shared everything I know about the business of self-publishing, with the sole purpose of equipping you with all the facts and knowledge you'll need to successfully self-publish.

In chapter one, we took an overview of the self-publishing industry in terms of print books, ebooks, and audiobooks. The statistics included there paint a clear picture that shows the book-selling market's exponential growth in recent years. The advent of new technology like e-readers, such as Kindle and Kobo, and phone applications, like Google Play Books and FBReader, has revolutionized the book production, distribution, and selling industries across the board. As a result, readers can easily purchase and download books of any kind onto a wide range of devices in minutes.

We also looked at self-publishing versus traditional publishing and the many benefits of self-publishing for authors compared to traditional publishing routes in terms of speed of production and delivery to the reader. When it's taken you a lot of time and effort to write your book, rather than wait on traditional publishers to accept it, which, as I've outlined, can take many months, self-publishers can have their books on the market in a matter of weeks. What's more, I've shown how, unlike in traditional publishing, the self-published author has COMPLETE CONTROL of every aspect of publishing their book. They alone decide how the content is going to be organized and presented in ways that are attractive to readers—and that will keep them coming back for more. It's you, the author, who decides the format of your book, the cover art, the final packaging, and, most importantly for sales, the pricing.

The chapter on pricing your book correctly to maximize its chances of selling well is, I believe, one of the most important aspects included here for your consideration. I've done much of the market analysis for you and provided a rough guide to help you decide how to best set the price for your book. I've shown you how to do your own pricing research by looking at books already for sale that cover a topic similar to yours and are of about the same length. We also covered the importance of registering your book in the right category so that buyers can find it easily, again increasing the likelihood of it selling.

Also discussed are the different pricing rates for the various types of publishing formats to ensure optimum sales. We examined the differing appeal of ebooks and print books to audiences and the increasing popularity of audiobooks. With all this insider knowledge now at your fingertips, you'll be able to forge ahead and set the prices for the different publishing formats you choose in a range that will appeal to potential buyers.

Of course, I've also looked at the third great advantage to self-publishing compared to traditional publishing—you, the author, get to keep almost all the profits.

In the introduction, I talked about how the reputation of self-published books, especially ebooks, has been somewhat marred by the huge number of poor-quality books on the market. I believe that recognizing that ugly truth early on could save you a lot of heartache later when your book fails to sell well or gets bad reviews, not because of the content but because of the poor manner in which it's been presented to readers.

You've made the first step to avoiding that fate by buying this book, and this will greatly increase your chances of sales success in self-publishing by following all the steps and guidance I've set out for you here. Throughout the book, I show the stages where I recommend ensuring a high-quality book by hiring professionals for editing, getting subject expert input, or typesetting your book. So, there's no excuse for not doing your best for your readers by producing a high-quality book they will enjoy.

Now, let's go back and reconsider the startling statistic I revealed in the introduction to this book—that more than 1.6 million books and ebooks were published in 2018 alone.[42] This is a great statistic to begin with when you're first thinking about self-publishing your book, as it not only shows you that there's a vast market out there but also that authors self-publish all the time.

We've looked at how various markets, especially for ebooks and audiobooks, have exploded in the last decade and are still growing. We've also covered the steady demand for print books, not just bought online but from big chain and smaller independent "bricks and mortar" bookstores despite the increasing popularity of ebook and audiobook readers. That took us into separate chapters dealing with the various formats themselves that are available to authors today when self-publishing their books. In these chapters, I've given you an insight into the size of these respective markets and the popularity with buyers of the different formats. We also had a close-up look at the costs involved in producing your book in each of the three different formats. This info will help you decide where the best profits are likely to be made when balanced against production costs.

In particular, the chapter on audiobooks gives you an in-depth look at this growing phenomenon that you may not have previously considered as a self-publishing format. You've learned about methods of production and financing to help you decide if and how you can benefit by self-publishing

---

42   Jim Milliot, "Number of Self-Published Titles Jumped 40% in 2018," PublishersWeekly.com, October 15, 2019, https://www.publishersweekly.com/pw/by-topic/industry-news/publisher-news/article/81473-number-of-self-published-titles-jumped-40-in-2018.html.

an audio version of your book. You remember what I told you about how you can successfully engage a whole new audience of non-readers by entering this increasingly lucrative market, right? So, whether it's print books, ebooks, or audiobooks, you now have plenty of helpful info and guidance on how best to choose a publishing format to maximize profits.

Talking of sales and profits, I believe one of the most important aspects I've shared with you in this book is to think of self-publishing as a business. This covered the different ways of distributing your books most effectively and affordably.

Lastly, having given you all this industry insider insight and knowledge to help you produce the highest quality book possible for the least cost, I'd like to wish you the very best of success with your self-publishing endeavor. You won't need luck as you now have all the tools at your fingertips to realize your dream of becoming a first-class self-published author.

Index

www.ingramcontent.com/pod-product-compliance
Lightning Source LLC
Chambersburg PA
CBHW032059020426
42335CB00011B/405